WHY MEN CHEAT

AND WHAT TO DO ABOUT IT

• *A Practical Handbook* •

Paul Blanchard

WHY MEN CHEAT
and What to Do About It
by Paul Blanchard

© World Publications
PO Box 24339
Tampa, Florida 33623
USA
Tel: 813-620-4517
Fal: 813-620-9096

Manufactured in Singapore

LC No. 94-070474
ISBN No. 1-884942-02-4

Thanks to Pamela Phillips for proofing this book and saving the readers from more run-on sentences than they will ever know.

Contents

PART II
WHAT TO DO ABOUT IT

Part I

Why Men Cheat

1

The Extent of Male Infidelity

"Are There Any Faithful Men?"

Vickey M.

Seventeen years of a bitter marriage to her childhood sweetheart, Robert, convinced Vickey M. of just one thing: "All men cheat."

Although Robert had been unfaithful even before their wedding, Vickey had decided that marriage would change him. But marriage made no difference. Robert continued to see other women no matter how much she pleaded. In fact, he refused to discuss where he went or what he was doing on nights he didn't come home. The fact that he had become the father of three beautiful little girls apparently was not sufficient reason for Robert to change his lifestyle.

When Vickey M. realized Robert was straying, in the first year of her marriage, she purchased mail order manuals on how to please a man sexually. She ordered nightgowns and teddies by mail because they were so risqué she could not bring herself to buy them in local shops, and she hid them in her chest of drawers so the children, or visitors such as her parents or in-laws, would not see them. She planned romantic events, bought her husband romantic albums, sent him cards at every opportunity, and even sent him flowers where he worked. When his birthday, Christmas, or their anniversary came, she lavished him with fine clothes and jewelry. All these efforts did nothing to change Robert who would disappear several times each month for the entire night.

I asked her to share with me the most painful examples of Robert's cheating. Vickey said Robert had actually been with another woman, a friend of hers, while Vickey was giving birth to her first child. But even more painful to recall was the evening she took the kids to the neighbors, made a wonderful dinner of his favorite foods, mixed his favorite drink, put flowers on the table, played soft music, wore her sexiest nightgown, and waited to surprise him. And waited, and waited, and waited, because that was one of the nights Robert didn't come home.

"You can't trust any of them," Vickey M. said.

I said surely there were some men who wouldn't cheat.

Vickey M. explained how neighbors' husbands made sexual offers to her, especially when their wives were at work or out of town. When she had just started working in a lawyer's office, the senior partner took her to lunch, then to his beach house where he suggested she be his mistress. Robert's best friend made a pass at Vickey M. at a pool party when Robert was elsewhere. Vickey M.'s father had even fathered an illegitimate child. Robert's father had left his wife.

"There are no faithful men," Vickey M. said. "Not even one." (Some women have stated this idea more emphatically: "Given the chance, ten out of nine men will cheat!")

Cheating is Hot News

Looking through the tabloids at the local supermarket, it's easy to come to the same conclusion. Famous country singers with alleged lovers, British royalty photographed secretly in the midst of affairs, sports stars admitting their AIDS came from romps with women who were strangers, presidential candidates accused of infidelity, long dead former presidents and their relatives accused of affairs with movie stars—these are just some of the headlines and favorite themes of the tabloids. Millions of tabloids are sold and read each month by a public apparently eager to learn that someone famous is guilty of infidelity.

Television and the local press have also joined in the sensationalism. In the presidential campaign it was considered proper for Bill Clinton to be questioned about whether he had an affair with Jennifer Flowers. Ms. Flowers had no problem expressing her viewpoint in Penthouse Magazine. One advantage the average person has when facing the terrible agony of an unfaithful mate is that no one is going to print it in the paper for the whole world to know.

Talk shows have brought unfaithful males into our living rooms to explain themselves. "Other women" have been interviewed, and there have even been shows about men who cheat with men. By the time we finish listening to what's on the airwaves or reading what's in print, we get the feeling the whole male world is cheating. Is that true? Not quite, but the truth is unsettling.

Four Women Speak

There are times when I have felt almost as pessimistic as Vickey M. One day I interviewed four secretaries at a small East Coast manufacturing company.

The senior secretary was in her forties and well-liked by the other women in the office. Her husband was older, had recently retired from the military, and just begun a new business in house painting. He had hired a young woman to assist him and was strongly suspected of cheating. When her husband came home at night, all he wanted to talk about was his new "assistant."

The youngest secretary, June, who was in her twenties, had lived with Ralph since she had graduated from high school. June once found condoms in Ralph's car—and she had been taking birth control pills. When Ralph came back from a supposed visit to his relatives out of town, she found two wine glasses in his suitcase, one with lipstick on it.

Another secretary's husband frequently went to clubs where women danced nude and lap dancing was featured. She worried he was now frequenting the modeling studios where beautiful young woman posed naked or scantily dressed. Although she agreed that what might be done in those studios was probably safe, she was beside herself at the thought that her husband, the father of her children, would go to such establishments.

The fourth secretary had given up on men completely after her divorce from an habitually unfaithful husband. She was living with a "female companion."

Visiting that office was very depressing.

How Many Men Cheat?

I had at one time thought that the majority of men are faithful, but recent statistics show just the opposite: the majority of men cheat.

In order to find out how many men are actually involved with other women, and the frequency, men have been questioned in interviews and surveys. If we are to believe the men, by their own admissions, a large majority are unfaithful.

The number of married men that have cheated varies slightly in different studies. Most surveys put the figure above 60%, but some studies show a rate close to 75%. Even a recent survey of men who called themselves Christians indicated that more than 30% had had an affair and a greater number had considered it.

Not only are an overwhelming majority of men untrue to their mates, but they are more unfaithful than women by a large amount. Furthermore, unlike most women, the average male is capable of having sex with a total stranger.

The average woman will have between five and ten sexual partners in her lifetime. A large number of men will have had forty sexual partners before they leave their twenties.

While there are woman who are unfaithful, and a few women who might try to compete with men in the number of lovers, most do not even come close. The statistics say that women are at least twice as faithful as men.

Gay males make straight males look like angels. The infidelity rate among gay males has been estimated at over 90%.

Cheating's Aftermath

The results of such infidelity are divorce, broken homes, troubled children, and domestic violence. "One day I simply decided I couldn't put up with it anymore," Vickey M. said, "so I filed for divorce."

When a man has strayed, it does not necessarily mean that a divorce has to follow. Some women adopt strategies of acceptance in which they remain in the marriage while unfaithfulness continues (only one out of four men who are cheating actually leave their wives for the other woman). Other wives successfully change their mate's unfaithful behavior. There are ways to estimate the chances of changing a husband's behavior. There are different kinds of cheaters, and different strategies for dealing with each kind.

As bad as it may sound when discussing such widespread cheating, life is not hopeless simply because of men. Remember, a sizable minority of men are faithful, trustworthy, and do not cheat. There is a faithful minority (25% to 40%) which means there are millions of American males to choose from. The difficulty occurs if you are already married to the wrong kind. There are clues a woman can observe before marriage to improve her chances of finding a faithful spouse (see Chapter Four).

It is important to understand there is nothing at all wrong with Vickey M. She is highly attractive, with a figure most women would kill for. She had been a loyal companion, a great housekeeper, a wonderful mother, and a great cook, all while holding down a full-time job. There are many men who would be extremely happy with her and never be tempted to cheat. If she can ever again take a chance with a man, that man should consider himself fortunate.

It is important for women who have been betrayed to know why men cheat. If women understand why men cheat, they will realize there is nothing wrong with themselves. In most cases they have not caused the problem and they haven't failed as wives. The problem lies with the unfaithful male.

Contrast the males in the lives of Vickey and Susan. Susan had been married to John for nine years when he came home two hours later than usual from the office. He said he had had to work late, but Susan felt that another woman might be the actual reason. She began to notice him leaving earlier and earlier to go to work, then staying later and later. She was convinced he was cheating when, in his sleep, John said, "I love you, -----," and the name was not that of Susan but of a mutual acquaintance.

John felt guilty about cheating on Susan because he came from a happy home and knew he was letting Susan down. Vickey's mate, on the other hand, came from a home in which his father cheated and justified it to everyone because "a man who works hard to provide for his family deserves a little fun now and then." While John had girlfriends before he met Susan, John had always been faithful. Robert had been unfaithful both before and after the marriage. John did not justify his conduct but felt it was a mistake. John was communicative and explained what had happened when Susan asked. But Robert kept everything a secret, would not explain his absences, and justified his behavior by saying in general that he had missed out on a lot in life by marrying so young and so deserved a little freedom.

The difference should be clear. Susan had a good chance to save her marriage, but Vickey's marriage could not be saved because Robert would not help her save it.

Cheating is a challenge to the relationship. In some cases it will result in a decision to leave a bad, hurtful relationship. In others it will be motivation for one or both partners to make changes in their lives in order to save their relationship. Some women have described the day they discovered their husband cheating not only as the most unhappy but also the most significant day in their marriage. If this day happens, there are a number of critical things a woman must not do if she wants her man to stop cheating or if she wants a chance for the relationship to continue. The things a woman must not do if she discovers her mate is cheating are so important we will consider them first.

2

Twenty-Five Things a Woman Must Not Do

When a woman discovers that the man she has loved and trusted with her affections has been unfaithful to her, the most common reaction is rage. In such an emotional state thinking is seldom clear, and immediate reactions can be dangerous. Because at such a time the future may look terribly bleak and hopeless, a woman may feel she has little to lose by letting her anger be directly vented. This could be a terrible mistake.

In later chapters we will discuss what to do if you discover the man in your life has cheated. There are positive, constructive steps you can take. But those rational steps cannot be taken until the intense emotion and feeling of outrage is under control. If your mate is present when you find out, tell him to leave you alone, seek out a trusted friend if need be, and gather control.

The list of things you must not do is based on several assumptions. If you desire to keep your man, you must not keep him by sabotage or dirty tricks. Whether you decide to maintain the relationship or decide to leave, it will help to have him think well of you either way. If you decide to divorce, large amounts of money and much frustration may be saved by keeping the divorce relatively friendly and out of the control of lawyers.

Other than giving a momentary feeling of revenge, it will not help if you do anything underhanded, and the price could be quite high. It is best to avoid doing or at least to delay doing anything which might further damage the relationship between you and your mate, your friends, your employers, and your families.

These are the things you must not do:

1. Do not act violently or make violent threats.

If you do act violently, your man will no longer feel safe with you. I have known women that so frightened their mates that they slept separately in a locked room, refused the food their wife cooked out of fear of poison, and moved out. If a man feels his life is threatened, he will make himself safe, and during an affair, this could mean he moves in with the other woman.

2. Do not act violently toward the other woman.

If you act violently toward the other woman, she may call the police. You will be unable to act concerning your relationship if you are in jail or under observation in a mental hospital. Worse, you may force your mate to come to the other woman's protection, thus driving another wedge between the two of you.

3. Do not act violently toward his pets or your children.

Sometimes in an irrational moment of anger, adults take out

their frustration on their children. This will permanently damage the relationship between child and parent. It may cause the father to move out with the children. Violence toward his favorite dog, cat, or goldfish will have the same result as being violent toward him. No matter how right you are to be outraged, he will protect the things he loves from your anger by removing them from the home. He may decrease his presence at home, or move out altogether. In any case, it's wrong to vent anger on innocent beings, especially those who cannot understand or protect themselves.

4. Don't destroy his property.

When Martha M. found out that Steve, the man she was engaged to marry had cheated, she took scissors to all his new shirts because she imagined the other woman had bought them for him. Vickey M. spiked the fourteen bottles of cologne belonging to her husband, Robert, so he couldn't use them on Saturday nights when he was shaving and preparing to go out. Another wife even slashed her husband's tires on Friday night after work. Not only did these acts in every case paint the wife as someone out of her mind, but they created further insecurity on the part of the husbands. Also, two of the three men made their wives pay for the damage, except Robert who never communicated with Vickey anyway.

5. Don't call his boss.

Since many affairs, if not the majority, begin at the office, woman often imagine that if they tell the boss, the boss will put an end to it. Many companies have written work rules forbidding fraternization, and other rules forbidding supervisors to date their employees. Even if your husband is a model worker, having an affair denotes instability to many employers, some of whom believe an affair clouds the mind of their employee to the detriment of his work. Not all affairs are obsessive, but employers who have had their own obsessive affairs will think all affairs are the same. Calling your man's boss may get him fired. This will just add more pressures to your life, and if you are considering divorce, it will make alimony and/or child support more difficult to obtain.

6. Don't tell your boss or coworkers.

If your boss gets wind that your life is in emotional turmoil, he may well decide you can't concentrate well on your work. It is an exceptional boss who can be counted on to think of your welfare and not the possible loss of efficiency at work. If you feel you cannot avoid telling coworkers or your boss, then be sure to stress that you are handling it well and it is not distracting you from your work.

7. Don't call his family.

If you call his family, you will worry them enormously. You may get his parents or one parent to come talk to him, and tell him what to do. Among other things, parents hate to see financial loss for offspring, so they will likely tell him to stay married. He will resent this intrusion into his life. This resentment will be turned back on you. Many sons spend a lifetime trying to establish their independence from their family.

8. Do not attempt or threaten suicide.

If you are serious about suicide, find emergency help. Vickey M. once confessed to her boss that she had a gun and felt like using it at times on Robert. If you have a gun, give it to someone you can trust during the crisis, while your emotions are stronger than your common sense. If you threaten to commit suicide, several things may happen. Your mate may worry about you and have you committed to a mental hospital for observation against your will. He may feel you are not as sane as the other woman. It may keep him on the fence longer, unable to decide between you or the other woman. If you want him at all, surely you want him because of your qualities and virtues, not because of your threats. Furthermore, a man who stays because he is afraid you will hurt yourself will always resent it and feel he has been tricked.

9. Do not appeal to his friends.

Because they are his friends, they most likely will stick up for him. They may feel that all the problems are your fault. When couples come together, often friends feel they have been pushed out of the way. His friends may not feel they are your friends nor will they have a particular interest in keeping you together—their interest will be in seeing him happy. Male friends often aid and abet a cheater, providing cover stories, meeting places, and even introductions. Female friends may well include the other woman.

10. Do not make an appointment for him with a marriage counselor, psychologist, or minister (at least not without asking him first).

While a marriage counselor, psychologist or clergyman may be of help, a man will resent efforts to make him seek counseling against his will. If he is religious, or thinks of himself as a very moral person, he will be extremely uncomfortable and guilty if he is contacted without his consent. At this critical time, understanding and communication are most important. Anything which will make him stop communicating or drive him away should be avoided.

11. Don't fake illness to keep him around.

Many woman opt to have that elective surgery they have been putting off as a way of keeping their man. Or they suddenly develop chest pains, dizziness, or fainting spells. These tactics will certainly keep the man's attention, unless he is very callous. But like many other less than honest methods, they will build resentment, and they will cost money which may or may not be covered under health insurance at home or at work.

12. Don't have an affair.

A natural thought is "If he can do it, so can I." A revenge affair will just give him justification, since you have done the same thing, and it may make him feel the relationship is so bad that there is nothing worth saving. Women who have affairs impulsively with a spouse's friends or relatives risk long term alienation. Woman who do this with strangers risk AIDS. And women who do this at work risk a complicating relationship and possibly their job. If your aim is to have a faithful mate, you must be faithful too. In any case the decision of whether or not to have an affair should never be determined by revenge.

13. Do not try to become pregnant.

When Joyce M. discovered her husband of fourteen years was having an affair with his new business partner, she stopped using birth control. She quickly became pregnant with their third child, but since Tony wanted no more children, the new pregnancy ended their marriage. Even if it temporarily saves the marriage, what do you do after the child is born? Do you have another? Do you continue having children until he is an old man? Many men will also resent this tactic and rebel against it. A child should be brought into the world with the consent of both parents, and out of love. A child who is a reminder of an affair, and a method of patching up the relationship, may end up not having the happy life he or she deserves.

(14) Don't confront the other woman.

This is very important when you are feeling emotional rage. In time, to help your healing process, you may feel you must meet the other woman. But the time to do it is not when you first find out and are highly emotional. The confrontation, which will certainly be reported to your man in exaggerated detail, may not flatter you. It will seem as if you are trying to make the decision for him, and the decision to leave the other woman must be his alone.

(15) Do not follow him.

Not only do men value their privacy, but this will also give you the appearance of being emotionally unstable. All the worrying and checking up on him will not stop him from cheating. The only thing that will stop him from cheating is a conscious decision on his part to stop.

(16) Do not become a nag on the phone.

Calling his office repeatedly, perhaps to ask him to bring something home, perhaps to report really unimportant news, may tell you that he really is at work. But it will not help him make a decision in your favor or make you well remembered if it doesn't work out. Alfred was called so often by his girlfriend, Maria F., that his boss finally forbid her to call at all. Alfred was the butt of jokes every time the intercom summoned him to the office for one of Maria's reassurance calls—and she called up to ten times a day.

17. **Resist the urge to reveal family secrets.**

Anger easily gives way to thoughts of revenge, and an easy way to hurt someone is to reveal all the embarassing things which you have promised never tell to anyone. "Spilling the beans" may give you momentary satisfaction, but once revealed, this information can never be hidden again. Often, these details may be as damaging to the wife as to the husband, but anger may give a woman the feeling that she "just doesn't care anymore." Revealing confidences is the kind of damage that cannot be repaired when your mood changes for the better and may result in very intense bitterness on the part of your mate.

18. **Put yourself in his place and don't do anything you wouldn't want done to you.**

When in doubt, imagine you have become involved with someone yourself, and that you are not clear what to do or not to do. When you consider an action, ask yourself what effect it would have on you if the positions were reversed.

19. **Don't run up huge credit cards bills.**

Eileen A. was married to a habitual philanderer. Every time she found something amiss, be it lipstick on his shirt or his late night arrival, she sought revenge the next day by making large purchases on his credit card. She was convinced this punished him and that it would put him under such financial pressure that he could not leave. In the end, however, it was more like shooting herself in the foot. When their marriage ended, she found that her husband was in such bad financial shape, with thousands of dollars of credit cards bills, that she had to accept only child support and forego alimony. If they had made up, she would have had to pay half the bills.

20. Do not make major purchases.

At the time Linda H. discovered her husband was having an affair, they were in the process of negotiating to buy their first home. She decided that if they had a home, things would be different for them. Buying something expensive or pleasing does not stop an affair. But even more importantly, it may cause the affair to deepen. Men who feel trapped feel especially trapped when major events happen. In fact, major events are a likely time for trapped men to cheat. Major purchases should only be made in times of serenity.

21. Do not make important career decisions.

While moving to another town to start over may seem desirable as soon as an affair is discovered, such decisions should not be made until emotions are under control. Some women, wanting to punish their spouse financially, have quit good jobs or asked for demotions. Such actions can be extremely expensive in the long run. Income and careers can be damaged while nothing beneficial is gained in return.

22. Do not rush to begin a crash improvement program.

Don't immediately start starving yourself because you imagine the other woman is thinner, or join a gym where you work out several hours a day, or take up a jogging program. Fitness programs may be helpful (provided a doctor assures you they are safe), but there is a natural tendency during times of emotional turmoil to overdo these efforts. This could be dangerous to the health in many cases.

23. Do not burn all the bridges.

Give yourself time to decide whether you want to attempt a reconciliation or not. You may not wish to even consider it at first, but a few days later you might feel differently. In the meantime, try to avoid doing things that will shut the door forever. There is a strong temptation to report your spouse's infidelity to your own family and to your mutual friends. They will, of course, console you and this is the kind of comfort that almost everyone needs at such a time. However, these same people may hold resentment against your spouse that will linger well beyond the time you have reconciled with him.

A man may not be capable of dealing with the hostility of in-laws and mutual friends. Faced with the strong disapproval of the people closest to him, he may decide that it would be easier and better to start over with someone new. Thus, by burning all of the man's bridges, you may make it far more difficult to resume a normal relationship, if that is what you finally decide you want to do. So, the best course is probably to be very selective in choosing the people in whom you wish to confide this very personal information.

24. Don't tell the other woman's husband.

When Gloria was driving to the store, she saw her husband's car parked on a vacant side street. Concerned, she caught Harold in an amorous embrace with the neighbor's wife. Gloria drove straight to the neighbor's house where she found the husband was home. She proceeded to tell the other woman's husband what she had seen.

As a result, the other woman's husband, instead of stopping the cheating like Gloria had hoped, left his wife. This made the neighbor lady available to Harold at all times, and made it impossible for Gloria to save their marriage. A little cooling off might have made a world of difference.

25) **Avoid con-artists.**

When Carol discovered her husband had a girlfriend, she went to a fortune teller from Santo Domingo. At twenty dollars a visit, assisted by tarot cards, Carol did nothing to help their marriage. And when her husband discovered locks of his hair, a rooster paw, and photographs of their wedding under the mattress of his bed, he was convinced that Carol had lost her mind. In a way, she had—because of his cheating, she had become desperate and was therefore easy prey for one of the many dishonest people who make their living by deceiving those with troubles and heartache. Cheating is not stopped by fortune tellers, witch doctors, potions, spells, or incantations.

There may be other bad ideas which can further harm your relationship rather than help it. Use care in all you do at this critical time to make sure you are doing what is best for you and your relationship in the long run.

3

Indications of Cheating

When a man cheats, or is about to cheat, there are often many obvious changes in his behavior which may tip his hand. Later, when what has happened becomes known to the betrayed partner, she often will remark, "I should have known," because the signs were so obvious. Often it is as if a man has tattooed on his forehead the message, "I am cheating." Some men make it so obvious because they want attention. They are openly proclaiming their independence. Some are guilty are hope to be caught and stopped. But most are just so obsessed with what they are doing that they ignore ordinary caution or just forget to cover their tracks.

Work Hours

One of the clues most often missed is changes in a man's work hours. He may say he has to go in to work early or has to stay late. Or that his job now requires him to travel much more, even on weekends, out of town with business associates (perhaps female ones). It could very well be true. And you don't dare ask his boss about it for fear of causing him trouble. If you will remember Susan B., one of her early warning signs was that her man was going to work early and coming home late. He was so anxious to see his lovely coworker, freshly made-up and dressed to kill, that he left his housewife behind while she still had the curlers in her hair. His affair took place at night, in his office, in the conference room, and at motels. Nights he was late were also evenings he took his mistress to fancy restaurants. On his so-called weekend "business" trips, he went to expensive hotels for getaways, including ski trips to Colorado and cruises to the Bahamas. Men whose business requires that they travel have a much easier time making room for a second, third, or even fourth woman in their lives.

Vehicles

Since his vehicle (be it auto, truck, or van) is essential to dating, in many ways he will start treating his vehicle like he did when he was first dating you. If he hasn't been keeping it clean, it will become immaculate. He may actually buy a new, expensive car which is beyond budget or a sporty car which is impractical for your normal needs, especially if you have children—a sports car or two seater, for example. In order to contact his new love he may install a car phone for "business purposes." Car deodorizers may suddenly come into use. Formerly disorderly glove compartments, side compartments, and trunks may become a model of order. The car may go through more car washes and waxings in a month than ever before, and he may spend his Saturday morning cleaning up his car, or even yours, if he has a chance to use your car for his affair. In fact, if your car is nicer, he may try to use it.

Time and Activities

You might notice he spends less time with you. You no longer get as much quality time. There may be movies he would like to see. Or special events he would normally attend that he no longer seems interested in—perhaps because he is taking the other woman instead. On weekends he might encourage you to visit friends or relatives without him. On weeknights, he might encourage you to participate in meetings and activities at church, in clubs and organizations, at schools, all without him. At least one inventive husband paid to send his wife back to college at night after she finished work in order to make time for his affair. When your vacation time comes, he might complain of his work schedule and send you off by yourself. And he might even tell you he needs time alone, and so go off without you on his own vacation. When you are together, he might absorb himself in hobbies or television to avoid having to talk to you.

Clothing

New found attention to clothing would be humorous if it wasn't so pathetic. Mates who typically wear blue jeans to work change to slacks. Men who prefer blue suddenly change their shirts to pink and mauve. Short sleeves become long sleeves. It doesn't have to be dressing up; it can also be dressing down. Changes in how he dresses may be to impress or please his new sexual partner. Not only may he suddenly buy more new clothes, when perhaps you did all the buying before, but he may also receive gifts of clothing which he has to present to you as purchases of his own. If he is dressing up, dry cleaning bills will escalate. Or he might actually be found ironing his own clothes for a change. Clothing may also disappear because he had to toss it out to conceal lipstick or perfume. Or because the new woman in his life didn't like the style.

Lovemaking

His lovemaking with you may suddenly change for a variety of reasons. The frequency may decline because he is too worn out from his mistress, or it may actually increase from either the added excitement of a mistress or the need to cover up the fact that he has one. There will be excuses if he is avoiding lovemaking—he has a headache, he doesn't feel well, he is too stressed from work, etc. He may suddenly introduce new variations into your foreplay and new positions or activities into the lovemaking itself, trying out with you what he experimented with when he was with his mistress. Or he may need you to do something really wild to get him turned on to overcome his lethargy.

He may begin to purchase sexual items or birth control devices which he never used before. In chapter one, you may recall June, who found condoms in Ralph's car, at a time she was taking birth control pills. Spermicidal suppositories, KY Jelly, or other lubricating products may show up. He may buy you a nightgown because he saw no harm in getting one for you when he bought his girlfriend one—or maybe because it serves to help him become excited enough to handle the demands of two women. X-rated videos, magazines, or sex toys may show up for the same reason. Nothing is more personal than your sex life, but sudden changes in it may indicate the presence of another woman.

Caution: It is important to note before going further that any one of the clues noted in this chapter may be the result of totally innocent behavior. Tension in a marriage often leads to jealous feelings and for a person in this frame of mind, it is not difficult or unusual to jump to conclusions. However, when the indications mentioned here start piling up, it is time to take a serious look at what might be happening.

Conversations

Subtle clues may appear which relate to your conversations, including the fact that you may have less of them. It is common for a man involved in an affair to stop discussing his life so that he is less likely to reveal his new activities. If he is involved with someone at the office, he may stop discussing work with you or sum up how things are going there with terse replies, like "OK" or "About the same" or "Hectic."

On the other hand, he might talk about nothing but his female coworker. Friends normally discussed frequently may disappear from the conversation, because if they are male they may be helping him cover up his affair, or if they are female, they may be the other woman. Many men simply stop explaining themselves or become uncommunicative. In some cases they will go so far as to pick fights so they can give you the silent treatment or spend nights on the couch where they will not be called upon to perform sexually. Your spouse may stop calling you from the office for fear of being overheard by his new lover. Or he may call you many times to convince you he is at work or on some important errand when he is actually on his way to see his new lover.

Gifts

Gifts can be a double-edged sword. Gifts may appear more frequently out of a sense of guilt. While you may love getting gifts, if he suddenly starts bringing gifts for special days he forgot in the past, it may be a sign of guilt. Since he has to give gifts to his new girlfriend, it may remind him, for example, to give you a gift on Valentine's Day or for Easter. Often men give the same gift to both women so if they become confused they do not have to explain themselves (the same thing is true about movies—they may take both women to the same movie on different days). Perhaps even worse, gifts may stop altogether because he is too absorbed in the other relationship to remember anniversaries and birthdays.

Finances

Affairs cost money—a lot of money. For that reason, it is easier for the well-to-do to hide affairs. If you are not well-to-do, the affair may create new, unexpected financial pressures. Affairs may mean motel or hotel rooms, flowers, champagne, airline tickets, cruises, gifts, new clothes, increased car expenses, and more. Credit cards at clothing stores may suddenly go over their limits. VISA, Master Card, American Express, and Discover balances may blossom. Your mate may even get new credit cards you do not know about so you will not see the bill, and so he can obtain additional credit. On the other hand, many men will not use a credit card to rent a motel room for one extremely good reason: a credit card can create hard evidence that an affair took place. So savings or checking accounts may suddenly be depleted. One man withdrew over $10,000 in one year from his retirement account, even though it cost him 38% in taxes the following year, plus penalties. To explain financial declines, commissioned workers may falsely say that business has gotten bad, and other workers may claim they haven't gotten a raise or bonus, or that their wages have been cut.

Eating and Diet

A man's eating habits can also announce his affair very loudly. If he comes home from having a hearty meal out with his mistress at some fancy French restaurant, he will feign sickness so he doesn't have to have a second meal, or he will pick at dinner and eat much less. If he suddenly begins a severe diet, it may be a sign he is trying to weigh less to get or please a mistress. Increased alcohol intake may mean he is nervous, and suddenly decreased alcohol use may mean he's trying to lose weight for that other woman. If you go out less, and when you do go, if he becomes only a salad or fish eater, when he ate steak and potatoes before—there may be cause for concern. He may stop asking for certain favorite dishes, either for weight control or because he is coming home too full. Frank, who consumed a nightly bowl of ice cream for over two decades, stopped altogether when his affair began.

Hair

Changes in hair sometimes are silly. When a woman has turned their eye, bald men may buy toupees. Long hair suddenly becomes short with weekly trimmings. Short hair is suddenly allowed to grow long. Stylings replace haircuts. Gray hair is dyed to brown or black. Mustaches and beards sprout. Pony tails and shags appear. It would be laughable if it didn't indicate such a potentially serious underlying problem.

Hygiene

Men having affairs may also make drastic changes in their personal hygiene habits. Deodorants will change and colognes will either appear or be changed. One husband, with a skin allergy to both deodorants and colognes, still used both, and would not stop even at the warning of a dermatologist. Teeth will be brushed more often, and those neglected teeth cleanings and trips to the dentist will now become high priority. Men who never flossed, floss with a vengeance. Men who never used mouthwash, or used ones that smelled bad, will now have minty green breaths, missing teeth will be replaced, and major dental surgery, neglected for years, will now become a priority, particularly if it affects facial appearance. The number of showers and their length increases, as does the number of shaves needed each day. Once again, he cleans and cares for himself like a dating male—which he has now become.

Personality

Changes in personality may also occur. He may become less tolerant of what he may see as your shortcomings, real or imagined. He may withdraw into a defensive posture, where whatever you say is viewed as an attack or investigation. His secretiveness may increase to the extent that he requires a postal box for his mail or a separate place for weekends where he has "space." Activities may change too. A churchgoer may stop going to church. Interest in hobbies may increase if he wants to stay by himself when home or hobbies may be neglected due to lack of time. An out-going man may suddenly become introverted or vice-versa.

Exercise

Exercise habits may suddenly appear or increase. You might assume he would be too tired for additional exercise but this is rarely so. This is because exercise is an excellent method of handling the stress of two relationships, even if he isn't trying to recover his lost boyish figure. He may jog, power walk, work out in a gym, learn karate, ride bicycles, or acquire exercise machines. This also is time alone from you, time when he can think about his lover and safe time where you cannot enter into his life with probing questions. Like many of the habits which accompany an affair, exercise is a healthy habit, especially if he has consulted a physician and is in good health. At first you may welcome this change, especially if he has been sedentary or overweight, and if this is the only change you notice you should rightly be glad. But if his new exercise habit is in addition to other changes like those already discussed, your joy may be short-lived.

Is He Cheating?

It is certainly possible that a man may make changes in any of the fourteen areas just discussed when he is not cheating. But it is unlikely that he will make changes in *many* of these areas all at once unless he has cheating on his mind, whether he has actually cheated yet or not. The only exception may be if he has embarked on a "radical" self-improvement plan.

You probably know your mate as well as anyone. You may know that the reason he makes a change in one of these areas is not cheating. It would be unwise (and unfair) to jump to conclusions. But if you have a funny feeling down in your "gut" that something is wrong, listen to that feeling, because your concern may be valid.

You may also want to read the following chapter before making a final decision. There are patterns in the background of a man which makes him more likely to cheat in a relationship.

The thirteen areas of change discussed above have been reported by many women whose mates have strayed. Usually several changes happen at once. The more changes, the more likely the man is either interested in some other woman and trying to be more attractive or already having an affair.

In addition, there can be physical evidence. For example, jewelry that isn't yours might be found in his car. Perhaps, like the husband of Susan B., he will mention someone else's name in his sleep. You know him better than anyone. If he has hated bowling all his life, but has now joined a league, perhaps you ought to find out why.

The fact is, that unless he is a practiced cheater, an affair is a dramatic change in his life. It is not something that is easy to hide. If you keep your eyes open, armed with the clues in this chapter, and with your own knowledge of him, you should be able to detect his interest and perhaps stop him before any damage is done.

4

What Kind of Man Is Likely to Cheat?

"Lifelong Indications"

By examining the affair of Angela C. and Brad, it is possible to highlight the items in a personal history which indicate that a man is highly likely to cheat.

Angela C.

Angela C. met Brad at a friend's wedding reception. She was immediately attracted not only to his boyish good looks, which included an athletic build, but also to his wit and humor. Brad was friendly with everyone at the wedding reception, especially Angela, even though he had come with another woman, whom he privately described to Angela as "just a friend."

The day following the wedding reception, Angela C. was pleasantly surprised when Brad called her at work. He had gotten Angela's work number from her newly married girlfriend before he left the reception. If Angela was free, he wondered if she could have dinner with him.

Brad took her to dine at one of the finest restaurants in the city, on the top floor of a tall downtown building with a wonderful skyline view. Angela C. had had very little experience with men even though she was twenty-seven, and she had never had made love with a man on a first date before. With Brad she was helpless. They made love in her apartment in the living room, not reaching the bedroom until much later. When she awoke, Brad was there.

Afterwards for a short while, Brad visited her frequently, almost every night. But after a month he had to "work," then he had to go "out of town," and then he was "under the weather," until he hardly called at all, or if he called, it was just to say "hello."

In time, Angela C. asked her newly married friend about Brad, and was told that Brad was "just a playboy." Angela considered herself lucky to have found out so soon, and tried to put Brad out of her mind, which was difficult since she had cared deeply for him.

Several years later, Angela C. ran into Brad at the opening of an art gallery. Brad was with another woman, but he found time to approach Angela, to say he missed her, and to ask if he could call. Feeling she was "wise" to Brad, Angela said it would be all right to call but not to expect anything. In less-than a month, Angela was once again deeply involved with Brad.

This time, however, Angela C. thought it was different. She took time to ask Brad questions about himself. She learned he had come from a broken home—that his father had left his mother. Through careful questioning, she learned he had had quite a number of lovers—that he felt insecure, unlovable, and that maybe he was so in search of the "right" woman that he wouldn't know her if he actually found her.

Unfortunately, Angela C. went after Brad with abandon. She tried to make him feel loved and secure. She did all the things for Brad that women have done through the centuries to win a man's heart. But soon Brad was coming to see her less and less, until she hardly saw him at all.

I tried to reassure Angela C. that she was lucky. She could have married Brad, and as her husband, he would have been just as unfaithful as he had been as her lover. "How can you be sure of that?" she asked. "Are men born to cheat?"

While men are not born to cheat, there are many things about a man's single life which can tell you the likelihood he will cheat if married. If you are a married woman, who just went over the list of clues in the previous chapter, considering your husband's life before you met may give you reassurance or reasons to worry. If you are a single woman, about to put your heart and emotions into the hands of a man you are just getting to know, checking these indicators may help you avoid a mistake.

Like all indicators, by themselves they mean nothing. It is the pattern of one or more of them, combined with the type of behavior in the past chapter, which can give you a good indication if you have a problem, present or potential, or if there is little chance of having a problem.

Brad C. had many of the indicators of a potential unfaithful husband. I felt absolutely justified in telling Angela he would cheat if they married. The odds were overwhelming given his background. Here's what I mean.

Many Lovers

In their discussions, Brad had told Angela C. that he had had many lovers. Men with a good many lovers tend to be more unfaithful. It is a myth that a man who has sown his "wild oats" will be ready to be faithful. It is a justification invented by men. Sowing "wild oats" is enjoyable for men, and even when they enter a relationship fully expecting to be faithful, they may miss their former freedom and variety, enough so they become unfaithful. A wide open sexual life before a relationship has been shown in many studies to have a very positive correlation with infidelity.

Previously Unfaithful

Brad also admitted to Angela C. that he had been unfaithful to a woman he had lived with previously which had caused the relationship to end. She was, in fact, the woman who accompanied him to the wedding where Brad had met Angela. Previous unfaithfulness is a strong indicator of future unfaithfulness. This is especially true if the previous relationship was marriage. If a man has cheated despite legal bonds and the threat of serious financial consequences, such as child support, why would he not do it in a new relationship, especially one lacking the legal and financial consequences?

Female Companions

Whenever Angela C. met Brad, he was always with another woman. At the wedding reception and the art gallery, Brad had been accompanied by other women, and Brad's "friends" were mostly women. An habitual cheater like Brad just doesn't have time for much more than the women he is juggling in his life, so he has very few male friends and hardly any deep male friendships. In reality, as Angela was to learn later from her married girlfriend, Brad was involved with other women even at the beginning of his relationship with her, both the first and second time.

Comes on Fast and Fades Fast

An habitual cheater will come on strong, spending lots of time with his lady, and fade fast toward the end. As he loses interest, and looks for another new conquest, he will make excuses. (Brad would have to "work," or had to "go out of town," or was "under the weather.") Getting him to commit to next Saturday night, for example, will be impossible once he is after another woman. He might not commit to a Saturday night date with you until Thursday or Friday, perhaps because he is waiting for someone else, or perhaps because he feels he has you in his pocket. If you truly care for him, you may waste months listening to false excuses, while waiting from weekend to weekend to get time alone with him, hoping to then discover if he is interested in you or not.

His Father's Attitude

Brad also told Angela he had come from a broken home. There are many different types of broken homes. What Brad should have said was that his father was an adulterer. Brad's father had told Brad that a man should have all the women that he could in his life. Brad felt his father wanted him to "try them all." A father's attitude is extremely important in the making of a cheater. If the father felt no stigma attached to cheating, the son will very likey adopt the same attitude.

Lies

Another thing Brad did was to lie frequently. The lies were often about such little things that Angela couldn't understand (at the time) why he needed to avoid the truth. One day she called him at his office to arrange a dinner date. She was told he had been out sick two days, but he had told her the night before how tough work was that day. Another time he told her that his sister lived in a different town from the place she where actually lived. In the first case, he had taken the days off to be with another woman, while in the second, he was readying an alibi for a trip he planned to make. Angela was concerned about these little lies, but they didn't appear to be harmful to her. She wondered if maybe she had gotten it wrong or if he had just become confused himself. The number of small lies added up over the span of their relationship, until finally Angela became concerned, but by then the relationship was over.

Drinking

Brad was also a drinker. When he came to visit, he always brought a bottle of liquor. His own apartment had a fully stocked, built-in bar. Heavy drinkers tend to cheat more than social drinkers or those who live an alcohol-free life. In part this is because alcohol lowers the inhibitions in the drinker, but it is also because a large number of women look for men (unfortunately) in bars, and these women also have their inhibitions lowered from drinking. It could also be that drinking is a response to a deep emotional problem of the type which drives many men to cheat, such as insecurity or a poor self-image.

Drug Use

Although Brad was not a drug user, drug use is even more of an indicator of a potentially unfaithful partner than alcohol use. The effects of many psycho-active drugs are not only to lower inhibitions but to induce the user to live out fantasies. Within the drug culture, casual sex with drug use is common, and sex in return for drugs is also common. Some drugs, like cocaine, increase sexual stamina and desire. A good relationship with a drug user is impossible because the drug user is by nature defensive of his habit and a potential danger to himself. Like a heavy drinker, the drug user is often using his habit to mask deep-seated emotional problems. The dependent, addictive personality makes for impossible relationships. Professional help may be needed not only for the drug user but for those who are close to him.

Unclear Residence

Although Brad had a job in town, an apartment, and friends which Angela C. also knew, there are some men, many of them married, who maintain more than one residence. These men may travel for a living or be very wealthy. They can often appear as "mystery men" whose coming and going may seem exciting, but they are rarely suitable for relationships. "Mystery men" get as much excitement out of their "secret" life as they do out of the affairs themselves. Their excitement may spill over to ladies who are tired of more mundane men and boring relationships. Unfortunately, a relationship with a mystery man is something like going over the falls in a barrel. While "mystery men" are rare, the more about his background a man keeps from you, the more you should worry about whether he will be faithful or not.

Secrecy

Many cheaters become confused about small details of their lives. They cannot remember whom they saw a certain movie with or which girlfriend met a relative or friend. They cannot remember which girlfriend they took to a certain motel and which to another. They get confused about many minor details. Rather than risk any revealing slip, they avoid discussing any details of their lives or your life with them. If they somehow slip and say something out of place, they will quickly cover it by saying something like, "Oh, that's right." The confusion will be even greater if the cheater is a drinker or a drug user. In fact, the cheater may try to blame his "bad memory" on his alcohol or drug use.

The Family You Never Meet

A cheater will not want you to meet his family for several reasons. They may reveal him by contradicting some excuse or false fact he has given you. They may also let you in on part of his life he is trying to hide. But most of all, if you discover him, a cheater doesn't want you going to his family. And if the cheater is married, protecting his home base will be a priority to him. This may be different in love affairs, but it is usually the pattern in habitual cheaters.

Would You Choose Him If You Knew?

My suspicions are that if a man told you up front that he had a large number of lovers, had been unfaithful to his previous girlfriend or spouse, had mostly female friends about whom you must not feel jealous, that he would soon be spending a decreasing amount of time on the relationship while making excuses about future dates, had a father who encouraged him to have as many lovers as possible, lied about little things, was a heavy alcohol and/or drug user, and had a tendency to keep the details of his life secret, you would have no interest in him. This is why cheating men make that kind of information hard to get, and why women usually get it too late. If you are not yet involved in a relationship, I suggest you make it a habit to ask about these things, hopefully before you get too deep into a relationship. A man who has nothing to hide should be happy to talk to you about his past, and these are just the kinds of things people getting to know each other ask and learn as a matter of course. But be very careful if the man will not discuss these things openly and freely. If you are already in a relationship or married and do not know these things, it is never too late to understand the man in your life and ask the facts about his life.

5

When, Where, and With Whom Men Cheat

Valuable lessons can be learned from knowing the answers to when, where, and with whom a man is cheating. It may be possible to guess the reasons motivating the cheater and judge the chances of stopping the cheating. By knowing when, where, and with whom a man cheats, it is possible, for example, to make a reasonable guess about the degree of commitment to cheating. When, where, and with whom is helpful information to have before making a decision about the future.

Although it has been suggested that the answer to "When, where, and with whom a man may cheat" is "Anytime, anyplace, and anyone," this isn't true except for a small minority of unfaithful men. Even before AIDS, men took care to protect their finances, primary mate, and family. The advent of AIDS has curtailed most cheaters to some degree, and certainly those who would cheat with anyone, although some men continue to take terrible risks.

When

The question of "when" men cheat has two implications. The first is a specific time of day or week. The second relates to a certain time in their life.

While the truly habitual cheater will be unfaithful whenever he gets a chance with someone who is pleasing to him, many men are not like this. Some men who would otherwise be faithful find themselves thrust into situations with someone to whom they are highly attracted. At other times, traumatic events in their lives bring out cheating behavior for reasons which have nothing to do with their primary relationship.

One Business Trip

David L. had worked with Kay W. for several years during which they become "friends" with a strong emotional attachment. They had become "husband and wife" in their working lives. Eventually, while on a business trip, they found themselves in rooms across from each other. The physical attraction, plus a few drinks over dinner, was more than either could handle. Fortunately for their spouses, David was a strong family man, and when the trip was over, he politely and firmly told Kay they had made a mistake. David and Kay's spouses never knew of their indiscretion, and the two marriages remained happily intact. This was a rare, lucky case for everyone concerned. But it illustrates the principle well that even a man "who has everything" can cheat under certain circumstances.

Scheduling Cheating

A man obviously cannot easily cheat during the time he should be at home. For this reason, most men who are cheating make time during work hours, shortly after work, or on business trips. Or a man may stop coming home when he should, stealing the time for cheating. It is a sign that his commitment to cheating is quite strong when this happens.

Vulnerable Times

"When" can also be extended to special times in a man's life.

When we later discuss types of cheaters, two types which particularly fit into this category are trapped males and men in mid-life crisis. The trapped males tend to cheat whenever greater commitment is required in a relationship. This could be marriage or the birth of a child. The mid-life crisis is by now a well discussed phenomena which most men seem to encounter if they live long enough.

The major importance about "when" is that habitual cheaters will cheat almost anytime they can with someone who is attractive to them (and with whom they feel safe in this day of AIDS). But there are many men who can be faithful mates most of the time except when thrust into certain circumstances or faced with a special emotional crisis.

Death of a Parent

When Bruce R. was working late one evening, his father called and told his son that he had terminal cancer. On the way home in the evening, Bruce stopped at the liquor store because he felt the need for a drink. A women who was not even his type was in front of him in line. Bruce felt drawn to her, not because she was attractive, or because his relationship was weak. In fact, his relationship was exceptionally strong. Bruce simply wanted to be connected to what he thought of as the life force. His grief at that moment clouded his emotions and his thought processes. Fortunately for Bruce's mate, his common sense overcame what may well have been a serious mistake.

Where

Although the habitual cheater may cheat anywhere he can get away with it, he is usually practiced in hiding his activities. Money helps the habitual cheater. Those who can afford it will keep separate residences, maybe out of town, out of state, or even out of the country. If not able to spend so freely, the habitual cheater will resort to motel rooms or borrow the apartments of male friends he can trust to keep his activities secret. Because the habitual cheater has been at it longer, he may raise suspicions but is harder to catch in the act. Likely, if he is caught at all, it will be because one of his "other women" finds out about his mate and contacts her. This can happen accidentally, so the truly habitual cheater is on guard to protect his home address and sometimes his true identity.

Men caught up in sudden, intense love affairs do not have the practice of habitual cheaters. They will rarely own or rent second residences. They are not as likely to borrow a friends apartment, and it may be difficult for them to get the extra cash to pay for a motel room easily without creating a credit card record. If their affair starts at work, it likely will begin at the office on a couch or in a conference room. It may gradually spread from there to other locations.

In later chapters we will discuss in detail the different kinds of cheaters. Swingers, for example, meet at safe locations, through ads in swinger magazines. When swingers trust their multiple partners, they will shift to homes where "club members" congregate or even "club houses" which are rented or owned by club members. Gays and bi-sexual males usually meet at gay gathering spots or "hunting grounds." Every community has locations known to gays including bars, parks, adult theaters, and rest areas. Gays seeking straight males hope to catch them weak from seeing pornography or from too much drinking. Men with fixations on certain types of sex may meet women through personal ads in magazines, rendezvous first for coffee or a drink, before going on to a motel room, or an adult motel which shows x-rated movies.

Often men with sexual fixations or compulsions seek out prostitutes who have their own room in which the sex acts are performed. Knowing where these type of cheaters meet often tells you directly what kind of cheater a man may be. This is useful information in reaching eventual decisions about whether to leave a relationship.

Other Answers to "Where"

Many men have acquired new rental property, a travel trailer, or a vacation home with the express purpose of conducting affairs.

If this happens combined with some or all of the types of changes previously indicated for knowing if a man is cheating, it may be another confirming indicator.

With Whom

Men who are practiced cheaters may be very careful in choosing a potential partner before pursuing them. They often seek out someone who has little chance of disturbing their home base. They are less likely, but still prone, to be swept away by someone they happen to meet. This is the opposite of the man who has chosen his mistress with his heart rather than his head. A practiced cheater, therefore, when confronted may simply drop the other woman who has been discovered. A man involved in a love affair is less able to do this. A practiced cheater is more likely to choose a single woman for his affair, while the lover cares not about marital status. If the other woman is married however, odds are that both marriages will not end in divorce, since only twenty-five percent of people who have affairs leave their spouses.

Because of AIDS, "with whom" has important significance in making a decision to stay or leave, especially if one values their health and life. The odds of contracting AIDS increases with certain types of sex and with the number of partners. If a man is a homosexual, bisexual, or driven to visit prostitutes, the odds of contracting AIDS from him are considerably higher than if he is a heterosexual cheating with a heterosexual woman. This latter type of cheating also increases the risk of getting AIDS, but not as much. The odds of getting AIDS from drug users who "shoot up" is also much higher than from the overall heterosexual population.

"Whom" Can Be a Total Stranger

How can a man have an affair with a total stranger? Many women are baffled by this. Most women would not feel safe having sex with a total stranger. Of course, some women do have sex with strangers, but they are very few, and usually they do not do this nearly as frequently as men. There are some interesting theories about the sexual behavior of men which may be of help in understanding, if not forgiving, such acts.

Women usually choose whom they will have sex with. It may not be a wide range of potential partners that they choose from, but within their range of male acquaintances who are available, women do the picking. Men, on the other hand, are not sure who their lover will be. They make offers which are accepted or rejected, and rarely get direct offers from women. Since men do not know who their lover will be, they fantasize about anyone they find attractive. By contrast, women usually fantasize about a particular man, generally their current lover.

Almost all men masturbate, and while doing so they fantasize about women they don't actually know, such as magazine centerfolds. In this sense, men have been making love to strangers their entire lives. This is pleasurable activity, which explains the wide range of "men's magazines." Pleasurable activity tends to be continued because of what experts call positive reinforcement. This means if it feels good, the behavior will be repeated. If it feels good over a long time, it will become deeply ingrained.

By the time a man is financial sound enough to have a steady mate, he may have made love in his imagination to hundreds or thousands of strangers. Little wonder that men can actually have sex with strangers when they have been pleasurably imagining it all their lives.

6

Myths About Men and Cheating

There are many misconceptions about cheating. Most of them make women feel very bad about themselves. Getting rid of the myths about cheating will help a woman to forget false explanations of why men cheat and concentrate on real problems. Here are fifteen common myths.

1. Men cheat because the other woman is younger.

While this is true in some cases, most of the time the other woman is pretty much the same age, or even older. As life gives us all experience, we tend to make friends and lovers of people who easily understand us. Large gaps in age do not make for communication—they make for communication gaps.

2. Men cheat because the other woman is prettier.

Men fantasize about women they barely know or have seen in the pages of a magazine. They fantasize about body types, shapes, and proportions, but most men seem to have a preferred type in mind. Because of this, the women with whom men cheat are often similar in many way to their own spouses.

Our society puts a lot of emphasis on "beauty." Beauty "secrets" help cosmetic companies sell products. Commercials put a false emphasis on appearance. Beauty is in the eye of the beholder, but chances are that the other woman is no prettier than the betrayed woman, different in some ways, but probably of the same general type.

3. Men cheat because the other woman is better in bed.

This is especially untrue for men who engage in habitual cheating. Skill and pleasure in lovemaking come from experience, from understanding the various wants and needs of the partner, and then practicing them to perfection, with embellishments and surprises. Because lovers are different, the other woman does not necessarily offer a man better sex, but she does offer him different sex. It is this variety which is often the source of excitement for a man who cheats. He has imagined himself with various strange women in his lifetime, and with a new women this imagination has become reality.

4. Men cheat to get a certain kind of sex they can't get at home.

While this is sometimes true, in general it is not the case. The vast majority of couples practice intercourse, oral sex, and manual sex. As regards anal sex, only about 20% of couples practice it. There are men so fixated upon a certain sexual act or fantasy that they seek out prostitutes to fufill these fantasies. These men rarely cheat with anyone with whom they could establish a meaningful relationship. Men like this, however, are a small minority. In the vast majority of cases, the sexual acts that the man desires are performed by his regular partner. If he cheats, chances are the sexual acts with his new partner will be the same ones.

5. Christian men won't cheat.

A religious faith is no guaranty against infidelity. If it were, we would not have witnessed so many television evangelists caught in sex scandals in the last decade or so. Scandalous magazine articles, confessions on live television, and resignations of top religious leaders seemed to dominate the news. Admitting his human weakness, a very famous and respected religious leader talked recently of sexual temptations, especially when traveling overseas. This particular leader claimed to have overcome his temptations.

There is some evidence, however, that Christian men may be more faithful. Recent newspaper reports state that over 30 percent of men who call themselves Christians have cheated. When you compare this with the overall male infidelity rate, which may be more than twice as high, it would seem your chances of getting a faithful male are improved with a Christian male. The pessimist in me wonders if any of these men said they were more faithful because they couldn't admit having violated their beliefs. But the optimist in me hopes that Christian males live a highly faithful life. Perhaps a religious faith in itself contributes to faithfulness. I am unaware of studies of other faiths, however.

6. Men cheat because the other woman is more intelligent, more fun, or has some desired quality lacking in their spouse.

When women have affairs, they are usually looking for some emotional quality missing in their spouse. It could be intelligence, compassion, a sense of humor, or another important trait which seems to be missing in their own spouse.

Some men cheat because of problems in their marriage. Strengthening the relationship can prevent infidelity in such cases. However, most of the men who cheat do not do so because of such problems. Men usually cheat for other reasons which will be explained in following chapters. Those reasons include sexual variety, deep childhood emotional needs, and opportunity. Many men even cheat with strangers whose emotional characteristics are unknown, or in the case of prostitutes and call girls, irrelevant.

7. He couldn't be cheating because he is such a good father.

Many cheating husbands are wonderful with their children, providing them with the nourishing time they need and doting over them. One wife said, "I just couldn't believe he was cheating because he was so wonderful with the kids," but a man's devotion to his children has nothing to do with his sex life.

8. He wouldn't cheat because he is such a wonderful man.

There are many wonderful men who have cheated. Some of these cheaters may be superior to other men in intellect, charm, and understanding. Throughout history the affairs of kings, emperors, and royalty are of historical record, and now the stuff of tabloid sensationalism. No President is more fondly remembered for his wit, charm, and compassion than John F. Kennedy. Eisenhower freed Europe from Hitler, and Roosevelt brought us through the Great Depression. Yet all these wonderful leaders apparently had affairs. The famous founding psychiatrist, Jung, had an affair with a patient. Charles Dickens philandered while giving us wonderful books, and the everyday wonderful male, who may be yours, is not immune to cheating because he has good qualities.

9. A man will cheat if he marries too young.

The assumption is that such a man didn't have a wide variety of sexual experience when he was young and that he will try to make up for this after he gets married. This assumption is not true. In fact, the opposite is true. The more sexual partners a man has had before he arrives at his current relationship, the more likely it is that he will cheat. This excuse is often heard from the wives of men who have married at an early age. Perhaps it is a copnvenient excuse suggested by their husbands.

10. A man will cheat because he buys men's magazines.

A young wife was distraught when she found a Playboy on her husband's nightstand. His possession of this magazine made her feel betrayed. She felt she must be inadequate if he needed to look at pictures of beautiful young women with fabulous bodies. The fact is that many men with happy relationships purchase men's magazines or outright pornography without cheating. And no, they do not buy Playboy or Penthouse for the articles.

11. A man will cheat because he masturbates.

Most men masturbate all their lives, beginning around puberty. Almost all men masturbate, unless there is a physical reason they can't. A man who says he doesn't, probably would not pass a polygraph test. Men feel tremendous sexual pressure during adolescent years when they are unlikely (and forbidden) to have a sexual partner. In his teens and early twenties, a male may masturbate ten to twenty times a week. Later the frequency declines with age. Mastrubation may be a safe outlet that keeps a man from cheating rather than a sign that he wants to cheat. Of course, it is natural to find all this sexual activity outside her control threatening to a wife, especially when the masturbation is aided with fantasies from the pages of men's magazines or pornography. Women may find this of concern, since they do not ordinarily masturbate with nude photographs of beautiful strangers. But masturbation during a marriage, with or without magazines, is not normally threatening to the relationship.

12. He is cheating because...

I am too fat, too skinny, too pretty, too ugly, too short, too tall, because we have too much sex, because we have too little sex, because I dress up too much, because I do not dress up enough, because I am too smart, because I am too dumb, because I am more successful than him, because I am less successful than him, because I have more education than him, because I have less education than him, because I am too nice, because I am a bitch...

All of us have qualities, good and bad, and all of us can find fault with ourselves if we look deep enough. Even famous and highly successful people at the end of their lives often regret that they haven't accomplished what they set out to do. They may feel that they have failed when most of us would have been delighted to have accomplished a fraction as much. For women, their good and bad qualities, real or imagined, usually have little to do with whether their mate is unfaithful. This is not quite as true when women cheat, because women usually cheat when they feel something lacking emotionally in the man.

13. He is cheating because he doesn't love me.

Many men love their wives dearly while still carrying on affairs. The man driven to prostitutes often thinks his wife is too pure to share the type of fantasies he considers "dirty." Many habitual cheaters come home to be wonderful mates, husbands, and fathers. Men in the midst of love affairs often go through anguish at the thought they are betraying someone who loves them so much and are torn by their conflicting desires for two or more women.

14. He is cheating because he loves the other woman more.

Habitual cheaters are afraid of intimacy, and love with a

prostitute or call girl is hardly possible for most men. Men involved in affairs may or may not love the other woman. For many men, sex comes first and love develops later. If he is having sex with several different women, it may be hard for him to develop deep bonds.

15. Because he is cheating, we will be divorced.

While there is certainly a strong relationship between cheating and divorce, one does not have to lead to the other. In some cases, a man can be stopped from cheating, and made to change. In other cases, a wife may decide that her spouse's many wonderful qualities offset his infidelity. He may be wealthy, or he may just be an man with exceptional personal qualities such as intelligence, charm, or compassion. Jacqueline Kennedy Onassis was married to two men who apparently were unfaithful, but she did not divorce either one.

These fifteen myths are not the only misconceptions concerning cheating but they are the ones which are usually the most hurtful or difficult for a woman to understand. Most other myths about cheating seem to revolve around two themes: 1. He is cheating because there is something wrong with his partner, and 2. There is something in the other woman which his regular partner does not have and cannot supply.

Hopefully, by now, you have realized that these notions are generally not true. If you discover that your mate is having an affair, it does not necessarily mean you have done anything wrong or that the other woman has something you lack. In fact, you may be a better person for your mate than the other woman in every respect.

There is also THE ONE GREAT MYTH. I cannot close this

chapter without sharing it with you. That myth is that if a man is happily married he will not cheat. Many men who are happily married still cheat.

Herbert C. had a wonderful wife and had been happily married for nearly forty years. Much to the surprise of his best friend, in a rare, contemplative moment, he revealed that he had had several affairs during his marriage. Neither his wife nor his best friend would have ever suspected that Herbert had a secret private life. His affairs had been brief and had ended without anyone finding out, but the memory had haunted him and apparently moved him to confide in his friend.

Men do not necessarily cheat only because they are unhappy. In the next three chapters you will learn that many men cheat simply because it is in their nature. Furthermore, society actually encourages them to be less than monogamous. Some men who cheat are indeed unhappy in their marriages, but the chances are good that many of these same men would still cheat even if they were happily married.

7

The Sexual Animal

"Some controversial theories"

People have argued for centuries about how much man is controlled by his animal instincts. Although the evidence is by no means conclusive, many people believe that man is not by nature a monogamous animal, and that it is instinctive behavior for the male to scatter his seed as widely as possible.

Many women find this argument offensive and quite reasonably point to the men who manage to remain faithful to their mates. They might ask, "If these men can control their instincts, why not the others?" Some women regard the suggestion that infidelity is instinctive as just a weak excuse for what they consider serious misbehavior.

To other women, the notion that cheating is part of a pattern of natural behavior is comforting, in a way. It assures them that this aspect of male behavior is not due to any failing on their part, but is instead, the result of an almost irresistible urge.

Indeed, some men have described their promiscuous behavior in that way.

Freddie C., a man for whom infidelity had become a way of life, described it like this: "The urge to find and become intimate with new women is more than just adventure for me. It has become one of the driving forces in my life. Sometimes I cannot understand it myself. It is such a constant and overwhelming urge, like the moon pulling the tide. Those men who cannot, or will not follow, probably live lives of quiet desperation. I just do not believe that a woman could ever really understand the power of this force. Just as no man will ever really know the pain of childbirth and no woman will ever really know how it feels to take a kick in the testicles."

If, in fact, the urge to cheat is driven, even in part, by this kind of biological urge, then it would certainly be useful for a woman facing this problem to understand the biological side as much as possible. For this reason, we will briefly discuss some interesting information which tends to support theory that there is a biological basis for cheating.

The Evolutionary Theory of Cheating

It is common sense that a man who mates with many women can have thousands of offspring, while a man who is faithful to one mate only is limited to perhaps twenty children at the most. There is a theory that thousands of years ago, the type of male who had the tendency to remain faithful and produce only a few offspring died out when the unfaithful males produced far larger numbers of their own kind.

On the other hand, a female who has a thousand lovers will produce no more offspring than a female who has only one mate. For this reason, there seems to be no advantage for a female to have more than one mate. In fact, if she has many mates, it is less likely that any one of them will stay around long enough to feed and protect her offspring. In order to insure the survival of her children it would be far better for her to remain with one mate and try to keep him faithful so that he is constantly available to help and protect her. So, over thousands of years, the kind of female who preferred many mates, produced children that did not survive to adulthood. Her kind died off.

According to this theory, what remains today are the highly promiscuous males and the highly monogamous females. If this is true, then there is a built-in conflict between men and women which could help explain many problems. Of course, this is just a theory and many people would reject such an explanation.

Monkey Business

Scientists study the behavior of man's closest relatives, the primates, in order to make educated guesses about the behavior of man. Obviously, observation and experiments can be conducted with these animals which would not be possible to perform on humans.

It has been observed that among certain apes the males divide their time evenly between trying to seduce the females under the control of other males and trying to prevent other males from mating with the females under their own control. It has been argued that this could be the origin of the human emotion of jealousy. Those males without jealous urges sufficient to protect their females from the advances of other males would not reproduce. Their females would be constantly pregnant by other males. For this reason the non-jealous males would not reproduce their own kind and would disappear over a period of time.

In the animal world, many species are not monogamous by nature. This is especially true among the apes and monkeys, the closest relatives of man. Orangutans make the rounds of receptive females during the mating season and then disappear into the forest without having any role in raising the young. Chimps are totally promiscuous and often line up five or six deep to have sex with receptive females. Monkey sexual behavior is similar to chimps, hence the expression "monkey business." Bands of gorillas usually include a group of dominant males who keep a harem of females whom they share with each other but from whom they exclude all other males. Among the apes, only the gibbon has sexual habits which could be considered monogamous.

The Role of Biology in Human Mating

Could it be that unfaithfulness in humans has the same biological function that it seems to have in the lives of other primates? Consider this. During the 1940's, a doctor compared the blood types of 1,000 newborns to the blood types of their parents. In a time of much more strict standards of sexual conduct, the doctor concluded that 10% of the children may have had a different father than the one registered as its parent. It should be noted that these tests were not sophisticated and that modern technology has not been applied to this situation. It is unlikely that such a test could be performed now in this age of informed consent and respect for privacy. And it is not likely that a woman would consent anyway if there was a chance that her infidelity might be exposed.

Whether or not infidelity contributes to the survival of man, it is clear that man is generally not monogamous. More than half of the people in the world live in countries where having a second, third, or even fourth wife is permissible and the taking of an extra wife is limited only by the husband's financial ability to provide support. Another, smaller part of the world (around

2%), allows a woman to have more than one husband. And statistics show that even in the western world, where monogamy is considered the ideal, as much as 70% of the men and 40% of the women have affairs anyway.

The Chemistry of Love

Recent research has revealed two more biological influences which may have something to do with infidelity in humans. The first involves research into the nature of sexual scents. It is well known that scents play a very important role in the sexual relations of many animals. These scents, called pheremones, are so powerful that males and females of some species, such as moths, can use them to locate each other from miles away. Pig farmers use extracts of these chemicals to send their animals into mating frenzies at the proper times for maximum reproduction.

The effect of sexual scents on humans is not fully known. Until recently, it was believed that when it comes to sexual attraction, animals like to smell it, while humans like to look at it. Thus the interest of human males in the female nude and the popularity of pornography. But, it is not yet fully known what role scents may actually play in human sexual relations. It was recently discovered that a small organ in the human nostrils is tuned to these scents. This discovery certainly gives more weight to the arguments that sexual smells have an effect on humans. And perfume manufacturers are hard at work trying to discover the secrets of these natural scents.

The other recent discovery that is worth considering is a chemical called oxytocin. This chemical may have an important role in human attraction and falling in love. It is believed to have a part in bringing on orgasm and may create feelings of attachment for a female. As a woman has orgasms with a specific man, the continued release of oxytocin may create an "addiction" to that particular man. On the other hand, there is some evidence that in men, oxytocin levels decrease with continued orgasm with the same partner, and that levels increase when partners change. If further research proves that this chemical difference between men and women actually exists, it may provide another biological explanation for cheating.

Studies of the effects of pornography on both men and women reveal differences which may be rooted in biology. When shown erotic films, both men and women at first show the same level of arousal. But when the film is shown over and over, the arousal level of women remains the same or increases as they begin to become familiar with the participants and imagine them as partners. Men on the other hand, quickly become bored with seeing the same film and the same partner, and need variety to maintain the same arousal level. It is possible, of course, that the differences shown by this research are not biological, but the result of differences in culture and upbringing.

Conclusion: The Biology of Cheating

To sum up, there is much evidence that biology has a role in explaining cheating. This evidence is not well explored and is discounted by many authorities. So, is cheating biologically driven? Perhaps. This is certainly not to say that a man cannot make a decision to resist instinctive urges. But many believe that a man's biology may be relentlessly pushing him in a certain direction. In view of how strong the reproductive urges are in all the creatures of the world, it would be unrealistic to not at least take into account that this force may be a factor exerting a strong influence over our lives. In this case, it should be at least considered in any analysis of male cheating.

8

Society Encourages Men to Cheat

Normal and Dysfunctional Households

A man who grows up in a "normal household," exposed to the "normal" values of society, may still be influenced in many ways toward infidelity. But it is a fact of life that many children do not grow up in "normal" households. Society's influence on men can be tough enough, but if the children are molested (about twelve percent of males are), or if they grow up in a dysfunctional household, the chance is even greater for an troubled adult life, and the many problems may include sexual promiscuity.

It is outside of the scope of this book to discuss all the ways a male growing up in a dysfunctional family unit might influenced. So in this chapter we will concentrate instead only on the influences toward infidelity which a child experiences in a "normal" household. However, it is still important to realize that a sizable minority of families are dysfunctional, and this can have severe consequences for children which will certainly follow them into their adult lives. Many children bravely overcome a bad start in a dysfunctional family, but others become dysfunctional themselves as they reach adulthood.

Raising Boys Differently

The literature of child development is extensive, and much has been made of the different ways in which boys and girls are raised. Despite efforts since the sixties to change this difference in upbringing, boys are still usually taught to be self-reliant and independent of others, and girls are still taught to be more dependent. There are, of course, varying degrees of independence and dependence, but the strongest emphasis is for males to be assertive, independent individuals. Behavior in this direction is rewarded in males and discouraged in females. Those of us who read the comics are well aware of Doonesbury's daughter raising her hand to answer questions in class but being overlooked in favor of the boys. It has been argued that this influence toward assertiveness for boys makes them loners, and in such loneliness they do not develop many of the social skills which girls develop. It is argued that this is not only the reason why males on the whole have fewer friends, but is also why men sometimes do not bond well. These theories hold that men are often incapable of sharing their emotions, because if they do, they feel their independence threatened.

In addition to being encouraged to be independent, to be "a little man," boys are also encouraged to be competitive, whereas girls are encouraged to be cooperative. This competitive indoctrination spills over into the types of games boys play and how they throw themselves into sport. Recently I saw a couple learning tennis together, and the young woman was perfectly content to keep the ball going back and forth. She saw this as the real object and enjoyment of the sport. The young man, on the other hand, couldn't wait to smash serves at her, or to angle his shots at the sidelines so that he could win the volley.

Women are discouraged from playing physically competitive sports such as football and hockey, despite recent progress. Women's sports are usually not nearly as well funded as male sports because they are not seen as interesting. There is a whole series of little leagues and pygmy leagues for boys, and girls are now sometimes allowed to play, but in general, girls are still not completely welcome in competitive sports. Encouraging competition, instead of cooperation between boys, tends to cause men to further distance themselves from one another, and contributes to the difficulty many men have in opening up emotionally.

Sex as Competitive Sport

Boys are often encouraged to think of sex as a competitive game. For example, they "score" or try to get to "first base" as rapidly as they can. Young men grow up thinking they have won something if they make love to a woman, and that the more "scores" they make, the more successful they are at the "game." Locker room banter among boys is sexual and often obscene. This is not just American thinking. In Japan, there is a club called The Thousand Kills Club," whose members document their sexual relations, and the object is to have sex with one thousand different women, in any way possible, including sex with prostitutes. This is really taking the notion of sex as a competitive sport to the ultimate limit. However, it would not be that surprising to find such an activity in the United States. Perhaps it already exists.

Initiation Ceremonies

In primitive societies there are often initiation rites when males reach puberty. In the Western World we may think of such rites as backward. Yet we seem to have our own rites of passage, even if they do not have the open stamp of approval of society. Many younger brothers are introduced to sex with the help of older brothers, including trips to local prostitutes or with the aid of some older lady of lax morals. It is common practice in Asia and in some Hispanic countries for young boys reaching puberty to be taken to houses of prostitution, sometimes by brothers, cousins, or fathers. Not infrequently our papers tell of some incident at a fraternity (frequently connected with an initiation rite), with a sports team, or in the military, where things have apparently gotten out of hand and one or more young women have been molested or raped. Not long ago it was reported that gangs in certain American cities required rape as part of their initiation. Our military recently embarrassed itself with sexually inappropriate behavior at its annual Tailhook pilot's convention. A pilot's unit at an Air Force base recently hired two nude dancers with whom a majority present had oral sex with at least the tacit consent of their commanding officer. Newspapers give plenty of examples of rich teenagers indulging in rowdy nights on the town that turn into "date rape" and "gang rape."

Brotherly initiations give the impression that what the young man is doing is fun for everyone. Perhaps such initiations turn out to be harmless for many males. But sometimes all parties are harmed. I was told of a young white man in a Southern town whose initiation to sex was to be taken to a mostly black section of town where a male prostitute was found to perform oral sex on the youngster. It is hard to imagine that such sex at the impressionable age of thirteen could not have had a harmful effect on the young boy, not only in a sexual sense but a racial way. This is not meant as a condemnation of homosexuality or interracial relationships, but a condemnation of forcing sex on a youngster by peer pressure, and leading him into sex which may not be his inclination. In this case, the ritual also included racial insensitivity.

The Masturbation Theory

Sexual urges for young males begin between the ages of twelve and thirteen. In many cases they have no forewarning of what to expect, nor adequate explanation. Erections occur many times daily, and will for several years. Erections can occur in a safe place, like in bed, but most males have had the experience of an erection in a classroom or another embarrassing location. This sexual urge arrives at a time when males are financially and emotionally unprepared for a relationship. Perhaps during farm days in less complex societies, marriage at a very early age took care of all this sexual pressure. But for the modern male at such a time, there is only one solution: masturbation.

Most males discover masturbation by accident when they have an erection and rub against the bed. Because it is enjoyable, the habit is quickly taken up. In puberty and into their twenties, it is not uncommon for men to masturbate several times a day. Many men masturbate during their marriages, and it usually does not threaten the marriage, but allows men to work off fantasies about sex with strange women without actually being unfaithful.

Masturbation, however, has an influence on the male's outlook toward marital infidelity. Because he is by his biological nature excited by variety, and because he has no clear idea who his sexual partner may eventually be, he will fantasize about any attractive female when he masturbates. He has already been initiated to infidelity in his imagination. Most boys can readily get access to the "soft" pornography of Playboy and Penthouse, and many can also get access to more "hard-core" pornography through their father's or older brother's collection.

This tendency to fantasize about strangers, and to be rewarded for it with pleasurable orgasms, prepares the male for many sexual partners. He is excited by any woman in a receptive posture who is pleasing to him in actions and/or appearance. Since the male may not have a lover during his teens, and may not be married until his twenties or beyond, his only dependable sexual outlet is masturbation and fantasies of sex with perhaps hundreds of women.

There has been much publicity recently about the effects of pornography on sensitivity toward women. Clearly pornography does encourage a man to look upon women as objects rather than as individuals. Some pornography is demeaning to women, much of it misrepresents how women are pleased, and some pornography clearly encourages aggressive behavior towards women. Pornography, however, will never go away, even if it is driven underground, and the use of pornography, apart from these negative aspects, is not necessarily evil.

The Father's Influence

The values of the father, or the male role model if the father is not part of the family, play an important part in determining if the young male will be unfaithful later in life. Boys tend to imitate their fathers, and if their father believes infidelity is normal, the son will often feel the same way.

Fathers and other male role models often believe that having sex is okay for boys. While females are protected and discouraged

from sexual behavior, fathers often smile proudly about the interest their boy shows in the other sex. Fathers often react positively and see a male as growing into a man when he has sex. There are even fathers who seem proud, or at least not upset, when their son has gotten some lady pregnant. In some cultures, having an illegitimate child does not adversely affect the male at all, but adds to his reputation as a great lover.

Esteem Among His Peers

Throughout life men achieve a sense of esteem from other males for their reputed sexual conquests. The pressure to report on conquests may lead to exaggeration and outright lies, or to an interest in sex with any available female. Young and old men joke with each other about sexual exploits, and men who have many sexual partners are often admired. In a coversation with me, one father proudly referred to his son as a "cocksman." Teenagers admire friends who were "studs." Married men declare that they are "married but not dead." While females take their self-esteem from being desired, males gain their esteem from being granted sex. The more sex they are granted, the larger the number of females, the higher their self-esteem grows. Once again I am not defending this practice, merely describing what happens and how it relates to a young man's attitude toward infidelity.

The Role of Pregnancy and Paternity

Sometimes the differences in behavior between men and women are attributed to to the fact that women can get pregnant through promiscuous sex, while men do not have this worry. With widespread birth control, it no longer seems that this factor is as much of a determinant of behavior as it was in the nineteen fifties and earlier. Differences in sexual behavior are also attributed to the importance of knowing who is the father in a system where a male supports his offspring until the child is able to make it on his own. There is no question that in many societies, not just the western world, the value placed on undisputed paternity is a major reason why men desire faithfulness in their wives, while they seldom practice it themselves.

Nature vs. Nurture

In previous chapters we have mentioned the possibility of cheating as a part of the biological nature of man. In this chapter we have discussed the effects of society on men's inclination to cheat. It is the viewpoint of this author that all theories of why men cheat are valuable because they help us understand that it is not necessarily a woman's fault that a man cheats.

There are still more reasons for cheating. Emotional reasons for cheating are discussed in the following chapter.

9

Emotional Reasons for Cheating

There are many emotional reasons why men cheat. By definition, emotional reasons are rarely rational reasons. Emotional reasons can be very powerful and dynamic. These reasons are varied, but the men generally fall into recognizable types. Not all types can be stopped from cheating, and some are hopeless. In such cases, a woman must decide if the man's qualities are worth the pain of unfaithfulness. But other types of cheaters can be stopped from cheating.

In order to know your chance of success or how to proceed, it is important to know why the man has cheated. Only by understanding the emotional reasons, and using them in your favor, can you hope to influence his decision to cheat or to stop cheating.

Habitual and Accidental Cheaters

There are certain types of cheaters who are habitual cheaters—these men may cheat throughout their entire lives. Like Vickey

M.'s husband, they seem "born to cheat." They are often unfaithful before, during, and after marriages, and also unfaithful during steady relationships.

The other broad category of cheaters are those for whom cheating does not represent a lifelong pattern of infidelity. The emotional basis for this type of cheater is quite different from that of the habitual cheater. Habitual cheaters are harder to stop than those whose cheating does not reflect a lifelong pattern of infidelity.

Rakes

To use a couple of old fashioned words which are no longer in common English usage, "rakes" are libertines who live lives of sexual "debauchery." Both terms have passed out of common usage. Instead we talk of "playboys" and "womanizers." The rake is interested in sexual relations with any available female he finds attractive and has the opportunity to be involved with. Some rakes also become involved with a prostitutes, while others hold themselves to somewhat higher standards.

The rake is not interested in changing his behavior. As one rake from Haiti once told me, while showing me photographs of his wife and mistresses, "I can't imagine waking up to look at the same pair of toes sticking out of the sheets every morning."

It is said of rakes that they have difficulty with intimacy. Each time they have a new partner it makes them feel wanted and attractive. Rather than attempt to build a relationship, rakes often prefer encounters. A rake is often wonderful at seduction, but poor in relationships. He can rarely be truthful about his nature, and he often changes relationships with little warning to his partners. Rakes will come on in a rush, then taper off their visits, often abruptly.

Often a woman never really understands what has happened. It is very difficult for the rake's partner to approach him about his infidelity because he has practiced deception and lied to the women in his life for a long time.

Mystery Men

One form of rake is what I called "the mystery man." A good example of a mystery man might be Howard Hughes who, it is said, had dates with two or more women on the same nights without the women becoming aware of each other by keeping them in separate suites on different floors of the same hotel. On the pretext of having to take important phone calls and attend urgent business meetings, he would excuse himself and shuttle back and forth between the two women as the night proceeded.

A mystery man may use assumed identities or variations of his name, maintain different residences, and usually must have a good income and travel a lot in order to mask his behavior. He may own separate sets of wardrobes.

Mystery men are often quite charming. They are quite practiced at their art and can provide wonderful romantic encounters. Some women find mystery men so intoxicating they are willing to put up with the off-and-on companionship. Mystery men are motivated by the sense of feeling wanted and worthwhile which they gain through their conquests. But they are also addicted to the excitement of their lifestyle, even though they are often afraid of being found out, and worry that doom is likely at any moment.

Even if doom comes, and the mystery man is caught, this does not deter his long-term behavior. He may apologize to his primary mate and swear it will never happen again. He may deny everything despite overwhelming evidence, or simply ignore the evidence his primary mate may present. But in the long run, the mystery man will continue to have affairs as long as the opportunity arises.

Swingers

There is also a small segment of the population whose members considers themselves swingers. These individuals wish to experience their wildest sexual fantasies, from threesomes through group sex, including orgies. Swingers usually meet through magazine advertisements or clubs. They often correspond using postal box addresses for privacy. While some swingers are couples, individual males can also enter the swinging "scene" easily. Swingers are not interested in emotional attachment, and consider themselves able to distinguish between love and sex. Because swinging has no emotional attachment, at least ideally, it often goes undetected and therefore does not lead to divorce as often as other forms of cheating.

Many swingers practice "safe sex," and testing for the HIV virus is often a prerequisite to joining a swinging "club." In a sense, swingers live for fantasies that seldom come true in reality, because not every swinger is the ideal they may imagine.

The Sexually Ill, Abnormal, and Sometimes Kinky

If you are judgmental, you may think any of these habitual cheaters are "ill." If you are broadminded, you might think "live and let live" and "whatever works for them" is okay. But there are habitual cheaters who are sexually abnormal. These are individuals whose development into adulthood has been changed at some stage so that they are not quite like the rest of us. In some of the milder, less harmful forms, they are the grown men who like to be spanked and told they have been naughty. In some of the more harmful forms, they are men who need violence or sadism to become excited. Often these men have difficulty with normal sex and blame their partners. Some men bring their fantasies home, while others who feel ashamed may take their fantasies to prostitutes or women whom they may meet through personal ads. Their behavior is compulsive. They seem to have no control over it. They may be obsessed about the behavior until they act it out. Often they feel the need to confess their acts, as further punishment, or to humiliate themselves. One might think of the recent case of a famous television evangelist who visited prostitutes, then felt compelled to confess in front of his congregation and a world-wide television audience. Often these men need counseling or therapy if they are to change.

(I have excluded from our discussions dysfunctional human beings, such as child molesters and men who physically abuse women. It is not likely that you can help such men by yourself. The safest, surest thing to do in such a case is to distance yourself from the man and get professional help for you, him, and his victims, all while protecting your own safety.)

Gay and Bisexual Males

Finally, in our groupings of habitual cheaters, I will include gays who are married or having relationships with women, and bisexual males. Perhaps these males are not "cheaters" in the same sense as the other types of people habitually involved outside their primary relationship. I say this because of the recent evidence that homosexuality is something gays are born with, not a choice they make. The size of the homosexual population is being debated—but guesses range from one to ten percent of the population. It is the opinion of many experts that gay sex preference cannot be changed. Gays usually become aware of a sexual preference toward their own sex early in adolescence, or even earlier, and this preference continues throughout their lives.

Mistakes

Thus far we have looked primarily at habitual cheaters whose behaviors are very difficult and sometimes impossible to change. However, under the right circumstances, with a person for whom there is an attraction, it is possible for a basically monogamous man to become unfaithful. This kind of man is very different from those who have led lives built around multiple relationships.

The man whose unfaithful behavior is the easiest to change is the man who cheats because he has found himself in a position of extreme temptation and yielded. Often this type of man feels regret and guilt, and he may never cheat again, especially if he does not "fall" for his new lover. This kind of circumstance can happen easily between coworkers on overtime or on a business trip. It can also happen between neighbors, in-laws, friends, and through chance encounters.

This is a human mistake, brought on by perfectly normal biological systems which create attraction, encouraged by society, and perhaps fueled by a desire to prove that one is attractive to the other sex. Such "mistakes" often happen over a few drinks, and may come as a complete surprise to both the man and the woman.

Love Affairs

The true nature of "love" is something outside the scope of this book. Whatever love is, it is not a rational feeling. Sometimes it leads to happiness, and other times it leads to pain. Some people feel love is a miraculous, uplifting force that can work wonders in an otherwise cold and impersonal world. No one would deny that love is a powerful emotion that changes lives and perspectives.

A "mistake" is quite different from a love affair. Many "mistakes" can happen without damage to a marriage. But when the word "love" enters the picture, something quite different from a mistake has taken place—emotions have taken over.

Although we all feel the need to be loved, the emotional reasons for loving and wanting a certain person to love us, are quite unique and individual. The reasons can only be found in each person's make-up.

Love affairs may be stopped for the same type of emotional reasons that started the affair. One person may fall out of love or one or more of the lovers may become convinced that the affair is harmful to them and/or their spouse(s).

Sometimes a love affair dies because it seemed like love in the beginning, but as the affair progressed, reality set in. Men and women having love affairs often "write a book" in their head which is the story of them and their lovers. An affair is an exciting romance that may lift them out of a boring day-to-day existence. But after writing a work of mental fiction for a while, they may come to realize that the reality isn't quite up to what they've imagined. On the other hand, if it's really "love," it may go on for a long time before reality confronts the happy lovers.

Trapped Males

Perhaps trapped males were once in love but have just fallen out of it. In many cases they got married to please others. One man said he was unfaithful because, "I felt like a prisoner with a one hundred year sentence and no chance of parole." These men have difficulty expressing their feelings to their spouse, particularly if they think it will hurt her. Changing a trapped male may require letting him out of the trap or at least providing him with more options, more freedom. Like other types of cheaters, his emotional needs must be understood and addressed.

A trapped male is unhappy with his life and would change it if he could. He is restrained from making the changes for reasons he may or may not understand. For example, some men remain trapped in order to raise their children. This is easy to understand. Other men stay trapped because of deep-seated emotional reasons they often are not aware of. In fact, they may need therapy to come in contact with their trapped emotions. Trapped males, who do not understand their own motives, may be hard to lure into discussions about their marriage for two reasons: (1) If they understand why they are unhappy they may be reluctant to tell others; and (2) If they do not understand, they may be unsure what to say.

Helping a trapped male may be an unpleasant dilemma for his spouse. If he is sincerely unhappy, she may be faced with letting him go for his own happiness. And keeping him may require giving him freedoms she is uncomfortable allowing.

Mid-Life Crisis

Affairs often accompany a mid-life crisis. The mid-life crisis, although once doubted, is now something widely recognized in our society. It is a period of introspection when a man questions the value of his life's achievements to date. In many ways, the emotions that feed a mid-life crisis are positive ones. Old ideals are often recalled. Affirmative changes in life may occur. As with depression, which often accompanies mid-life crisis, the pain becomes so uncomfortable that changes must be made for happiness to return.

The duration of a mid-life crisis varies greatly. But since it is a painful experience, the person undergoing the crisis is moved to solve it. The crisis may solve itself in ways that keep a marriage together or pull it apart. A mid-life crisis is an internal event with external effects in the lives of all those close to the person experiencing the crisis. How it may affect a wife varies. A wife who finds herself in danger of losing her marriage will need to carefully understand how her mate feels and where he is headed in life. It is only by using understanding of what is motivating the crisis that she can reach decisions about her own life or hope to influence the outcome of the crisis.

Halfway There

It is hoped that the first half of this book has helped to explain why men cheat. It is also hoped that the reader has gained background information which can be helpful in making decisions about whether to end a relationship, whether to tolerate cheating, or whether to attempt to change a man's unfaithful behavior. If a woman has read the first half of this book correctly, she should feel better about herself, and understand that, most likely, she was not responsible for causing her spouse to cheat.

The second half of this book is about taking action. It is designed to help a woman take charge of her life and make sound decisions about her relationship after cheating has occurred.

PART II

WHAT TO DO
ABOUT IT

The following pages will help you create a plan of action, suited to your own individual needs. In addition to solving problems, taking positive action will help to heal depression and make you feel better about yourself. Use as much of this material as you feel will be useful.

10

Gather Your Supporters

When a woman first discovers or suspects that the man in her life is cheating, she should first refer to chapter two of this book for those actions she absolutely must not take. It is quite natural to be outraged, and for feelings to be out of control. However, irrational actions will not help to solve the problem, and can in fact make the problem much worse. It is better to attempt to follow a carefully considered plan of action.

The first positive step in dealing with infidelity is gathering supporters. You will need to identify your support group. Cheating is a major crisis, and there is no need to go through such a crisis by yourself.

There are several reasons for gathering a support group.

The group will help you cope emotionally. It will steer you on a constructive course of action. It will help you reach such decisions as whether to keep the relationship or abandon it. If you decide to attempt to change the cheating behavior, the support group will help you decide what strategy to take.

A Reliable Advisor

There should be one member of the support group whose opinion and intellect you trust sufficiently to give you the best impartial advice. That person might be called your Reliable Advisor. You might think of the Reliable Advisor as a filter who listens to everything said by you and your support group and then gives advice or make comments about the evaluations you have made and the actions you contemplate taking.

You may wish to think of your Reliable Advisor as a buddy, friend, ally, big sister, or brother. But be careful. Your Reliable Advisor should like and care about you, but it is not necessary that he or she have a deep emotional attachment to you.

In fact, that might get in the way of getting honest, effective advice. The qualities you want in a Reliable Advisor are -

(1) A good orderly mind,
(2) The ability to listen,
(3) A keen intellect, and
(4) Broad life experience.

Relationship Counselor

During such a crisis, one should not do without a mental health counselor who specializes in relationship and marriage counseling. Counselors can be helpful in whatever may happen, from making up to breaking up, including sticking it out.

Even without a crisis, using a counselor to the extent you need is a good idea. The counselor used will likely be a psychologist since the trend is for psychiatrists to deal more exclusively with serious mental illness. In some states, it is possible to become a counselor without being a psychologist. This fact makes it even more important to use care in selecting the right person. Many insurance companies no longer pay for what they see as "routine" and non-prescribed counseling. Financially you may not feel able to afford a counselor. Sometimes this can be penny-wise and pound-foolish.

More often than not, the counselor becomes the Reliable Advisor. But this does not necessarily have to be so. And in the day of insurance limitations, it may not be practical to use a professional counselor from the beginning of the crisis until it is resolved. Counselors tend to make good Reliable Advisors because they have a lot of life experience, have heard just about everything, have the ability to listen well, and usually have keen intellect. An orderly mind is a different matter.

If you do not know where to find a counselor, you can usually get a list of a large number of references from friends, medical doctors, or from the local mental health association. If you do not like the counselor, change. As with any profession, there are competent counselors and less than competent counselors. Experience varies. So does the rate of success.

Relationship counseling has taken quite a beating in the public eye. It has been said there has been a proliferation of counselors but no significant decrease in divorce or any measurable evidence that happiness has been improved. This is a somewhat valid criticism. Remember, however, that counseling may lead to divorce, as some relationships should not be kept because they are too harmful. In these cases, counselors assist in rebuilding torn and damaged lives, and it is in such cases that they are needed even more.

Best Friends

When there are crisis in our lives, everyone wants their best friend involved. Best friends usually do their most important work by just listening and understanding. A best friend does not usually make a good Reliable Advisor. A best friend may be outraged to such a degree that he or she may not be able to give effective advice. We don't necessarily chose our best friends for orderly minds, keen intellects, or broad life experiences. In fact, we often pick our best friends (or they pick us) because they accept us, warts and all. This is not a time of life when one wants sugar coated opinions on improving yourself, your relationship, or whether to end your relationship. Perhaps your best friend can be your Reliable Advisor, if he or she is also an exceptional person, but before you automatically select them for such a role, you might want to give it some thought.

Relatives

Relatives who will be supportive, not critical, are needed in your support group. But it is often impossible to tell close relatives the truth about cheating without making reconciliation more difficult. Therefore, weigh including them carefully. Sometimes relatives qualify as Reliable Advisors, but usually they do not. Relationships between father and child, and mother and child, are very complex and often difficult in themselves. A hot-headed father will rush in to protect his little girl. A critical mother will tell her little girl it is all her fault. More distant relatives might be helpful - respected aunts or uncles, for example - if they can keep a secret from Mom and Dad.

Clergy

Many religious people use clergy for their counselors and Reliable Advisors. In turn, the clergy often refer their parishioners in such cases to professional mental health counselors. Certainly a friendly clergyman who can be supportive without interfering will be helpful to you in your support group. However, it is important that you know the clergyman well enough to be sure that he would have a helpful attitude.

Support Groups

There are support groups at local women's centers, and through mental health associations, and some hospitals and churches. In support groups such as these, a woman may meet other women in similar circumstances. She may learn from them. Sometimes, because of shyness or the emotional difficulty of speaking out about what has happened, women run away from such groups at first. If you are lucky enough to have such a support group available, use it. It may be very helpful.

It is unlikely you can pick someone to be a Reliable Advisor from such a support group. The members are there to overcome their own hurts. But you can gather support and ideas. You can get opinions about your own ideas which have the voice of experience behind them.

Employers

It may be necessary to include your boss in your support group if you need time off for counseling or group meetings. If it is not necessary, do not do it. Your employer cannot help but see you as an employee in an emotional crisis who cannot function as productively as before and he may be correct about this. There is no reason to risk your job. Because things confided to fellow employees have a way of getting back to the boss, it is best to "leave your problems home" to the extent possible. There are exceptions, but in general it is not worth risking your employment.

Other Friends and Acquaintances

If you do not pick a counselor to be a Reliable Advisor, or if you cannot afford to keep one during the duration of your decision making process, the most likely place to find a Reliable Advisor will be among your friends and other acquaintances. This candidate to be your Reliable Advisor will probably be someone you admire and hold in high esteem. You will need to talk to them, explain what has happened, and ask them if they will help. Many people are surprised when they are asked to help because they often think the other person would not be interested in their advice. But often when someone is told their advice is valued, they will be flattered and willing to help. Let them know their advice will never be discussed with your spouse, and keep this promise.

Reality Checks

In deciding what to do about cheating, a woman will make many inventories. She will check out herself, her relationship, and decide whether to make an effort to stop the cheating, whether to ignore it, or whether to leave the relationship. It is important that at every step of the way, there is confirmation. A Reliable Advisor provides "reality checks" about your opinion of yourself, your relationship, and your course of action.

Two Can Be Better Than One

You may ask, if it is a good idea to have one Reliable Advisor, might it be even better to have two? The answer is: have as many advisors as it takes for you. Just don't get confused or become inactive because of contradictory advice. You can have duplicate support groups, more than one counselor, include more than one friend, relative, or clergyman. Whatever helps you to find peace and make wise decisions is what you need.

Male and Female Advisors

It is possible to have both a male and a female Reliable Advisor. Some women find it very helpful to have a man's point of view, as it is hard for them to understand the male perspective about things like cheating. There are some exceptional men who actually qualify as feminists, who are compassionate, understanding, and most helpful in such a crisis. You will be lucky if you know both a man and a woman you can rely on for advice.

Warning!

Too often, embarrassed and feeling they have done something wrong, women do not seek out comfort or advice. Withdrawing will not make the problem go away. It will not make you feel better. There is nothing to feel embarrassed about in having an unfaithful mate. It happens to most women, whether they know it or not. Most likely, nothing you have done has contributed to his cheating. But if it has, you will want to know about it, so you can change it. Do not let your normal feelings of embarrassment keep you from the assistance and advice you now need to change your world and perhaps the actions of your mate. Seek out a support group, identify your Reliable Advisor, and make an inventory of yourself, your relationship, and your finances, before deciding on a course of action.

11

Evaluating Yourself: The Possibility for Self-Improvement

Many women see infidelity not only as an unpleasant reality, but a reality that has to be dealt with. Learning that a mate is unfaithful can become a challenge to better yourself, your relationship, or to make a new life without the relationship.

Before these things can be done, you will need to take an honest look at yourself.

It is a good idea to have a notebook to jot down items to discuss with your support group and particularly with your Reliable Advisor. In this way ideas won't be forgotten. Some woman also like to use diaries to write out their feelings. This can be a good tool for venting anger. Notebooks and diaries should not be written with the idea of later showing them to the unfaithful partner. This will tempt you to write to him instead of to yourself. Your mate should never see your diary and notebook. A good mate will respect your privacy, but you may need to enforce this by hiding it in a spot where he cannot easily find it.

In time, an inventory of the relationship will be made, but it is best to start with yourself. Your self-inventory will help you identify areas of improvement, but perhaps more importantly, it may rid you of negative, distorted, and hurtful views of yourself. When there are things to change, making changes will let you know you are taking control of your life and taking positive action. "I felt as if I was putting my life back in my own hands," as one woman told me. "The day I learned he was cheating changed my life. It may have been the most important day of my life."

Summing Yourself Up

List in the notebook, as soon as you are able, without taking too much time to reflect, your good qualities and those needing change. Summing up your good qualities will help you to feel good about yourself. Summing up those you think need changing will give you items to double check for reality with your Reliable Advisor and other members of your support group. When you run both lists by those in your support group, ask them to add or subtract from them if they can. Listen to their advice and delete those items from the list they do not agree with. They are probably false views of yourself if your friends, support group, and Reliable Advisor do not feel they are true.

Things Woman Often Want to Change

The most common fault women find with themselves is that they are overweight. I once was at an office Christmas party where New Year's resolutions were revealed. Every woman at the party resolved to lose weight in the following year, including several with figures other women will kill for, and body fat levels bordering on 10%. It is common for women to think they are overweight in our culture because boyish type models seem to dominate advertising. Men, however, are rarely turned on by bodies like Twiggy's. It is common to think the man is cheating because you are overweight, but unless you are really obese, this is rarely the case. Men with very obese women may avoid sex with them and cheat elsewhere. But the obesity must be really significant. One good judge of whether you are overweight or not can be the family physician. Your physician can accurately advise if you are overweight, any potential threat to your health, and a sensible diet and exercise plan, but neither should be started without consulting a doctor, and probably having a physical.

It is common for women to find other faults with their bodies, real or imagined. There is no evidence at all to support the idea that men cheat because a woman does not have large breasts. Breast size plays a minor part in attraction and stimulation for some men. But it would be an extremely rare case for a man to cite breast size as a reason for cheating.

As part of the natural aging process, the bodies of men and women become less taut and more wrinkled. Diet can help here. And exercise. There are many forms of exercise which can be helpful. Pick one, be it jogging, swimming, biking, walking, working out in a gym, aerobics, or organized sports such as tennis and racquetball. An exercise habit is healthy and can only do you good, but it should not be begun without checking with your doctor. Good exercise programs usually contain changes in your diet to match the type of activity you take up. Exercise is also important because it is an excellent way of working off the tension, anger, and anxiety you may feel during the difficult crises of infidelity. They key to a good exercise program is keeping up the habit at least several days a week. Once the habit is established, most people don't feel quite right if they skip a workout.

Some individuals go through life with deep-seated problems which are unresolved. They are generally unhappy in one way or another. In some cases they are depressed, sometimes severely so.

This depression or chronic unhappiness can have a very detrimental effect on a relationship. People suffering from these problems need to work out their difficulties with a professional counselor and sometimes may need medication. They may start with a visit to a psychiatrist. There is no reason to go through every day feeling unhappy when modern medicines and talking it over can improve the quality of life. If you feel you have always been unhappy, even before any potential infidelity, then by all means do not deny yourself. Usually these 'ypes of treatment are covered by insurance.

Cosmetic Surgery

Countless women have had face lifts, tummy tucks, and liposuction in the hopes this will restore youth or beauty and keep a husband at home or help to find a new one. There are many women who feel a man should accept a woman for what she is and that a woman should not risk her health and appearance. On the other hand, there are many women who feel better about themselves and more confident because they straightened teeth, removed an overbite, enlarged their breasts, or did some other form of cosmetic surgery. Many of these women are more motivated about feeling good about themselves than by attracting or pleasing a man. Elective surgery of any kind should only be undertaken after careful consideration and complete research. Elective, cosmetic surgery is rarely covered under insurance unless it involves a more serious problem.

When Rita R. found out her husband had been unfaithful, she promptly made plans to have her breasts enlarged. Rita said she had always wanted the surgery because she was really very flat with no noticeable breasts. It had made her feel self-conscious all her life. Their marriage did not last, but Rita consoles herself that at least her husband paid for the enlargement of her breasts which now gives her more confidence and makes her feel more attractive to men.

Husbands often oppose cosmetic surgery. Perhaps this is because they are concerned for the safety of their wife and the expense involved. But often it is because they do not want the woman to change, gain more confidence, or be more attractive. This was true of Rita's husband. Such husbands see improvements in wife's body or life as threatening.

Education

Debbie P. found in making her personal inventory that she felt uneducated. Her spouse was having a love affair, which he constantly denied, at work. If Debbie spoke to him about it, he was sullen, and the affair continued no matter what Debbie did. First she completed her high school diploma - Debbie had dropped out of school after becoming pregnant. Next, she went to the junior college, and then to the local university, achieving a four year degree in journalism. Although her husband in time abandoned his affair, in the end Debbie left him, content with her new interests, high-paying career, and the friends she had made through the university.

Volunteer Work

Although society is just learning to deeply appreciate the value of being a housewife, many housewives feel the need of something else in their life, particularly when coping with an unfaithful spouse. Debbie P. filled that void through education, but other women have found new interests in volunteer work. If you have time for such work, you can perform a wonderful service while making new friends and acquiring new interests. Volunteers are needed by churches, mental health centers, hospitals, civic organizations, political clubs, and a variety of organizations from scouts to big sister groups, from ethnic associations to flower clubs. If this helps you gain self-esteem, and it helps others, why not do it?

Smoking

Many smokers resolve to quit after they make their personal inventory. Others feel it is too stressful to quit while having personal problems in their life. Actually, quitting at times of ultimate stress can give confidence that the person will not start again during less stressful times. Only tobacco companies still maintain that smoking is harmless or that individuals have a right to ruin their health. Only tobacco companies deny there is any danger from second hand smoke to children. Smoking adversely affects appearance by yellowing teeth and fingers. Smoking often creates an unpleasant odor in one's clothing and hair. Smoking makes the breath unpleasant, and has been shown to contribute to premature wrinkling of the skin. Also, smoking masks over sex pheremones - those unnoticed but natural sexual scents that aid in attraction.

Smoking overall does more harm to a woman's appearance than a few extra pounds most women think they may gain. Not every ex-smoker gains weight, and those that do find ways to lose it.

Alcohol Use

Quitting alcohol is something that frequently pops up in the list of things to change. It is a common experience among women who have discovered their mate is unfaithful to drink until they pass out. This solves nothing - the next day their mate is still unfaithful, and they feel awful. Alcohol isn't a good way to handle stress. It often blurs the problem, and creates a false feeling that everything is fine when it isn't. It suppresses dreaming, in which we often work out our emotional problems on a subconscious level. There is conflicting evidence about alcohol use on our health in moderate amounts. But generally alcohol use is unhealthy. The extra calories contribute to weight problems, and it has been suggested drinking is linked to breast cancer. Woman who are habitual drinkers may find their drinking out of control during emotionally stressful periods. They may need to deal with alcohol abuse before they can effectively cope with any other problem in their life.

Drug Use

If drug use is in your inventory of bad habits, stop. If you cannot stop, get professional help. Even "earth people" should give up their drug habits because someday they will be surprised to find themselves in trouble. Someone with a drug addiction cannot live a happy life until they stop the substance abuse. In fact, depending on the drug, they may not live at all. I have known desperate young women who abandoned their children and sold their bodies in order to maintain a drug habit. They never thought they would be in such a position when they started using drugs. Just like alcohol use, drug abuse can get out of control during an emotional crisis. Someone with a drug problem has to deal with that problem before they can possibly solve their relationship problems. They are kidding themselves if they think a healthy relationship can include drug abuse.

Set Your Own Pace

Unless you are a perfect individual, a review of your good and bad points should give you something to change or improve upon. It is important to act on this, to take some charge over your life. The change may or may not have anything to do with your mate.

Your changes may include nothing discussed above but instead something that uniquely fits your life.

Whatever changes you decide to make for your positive self image, do them at your own pace. You do not have to do everything at once. Like with his cheating, you must deal with it in your own time, at your own pace. This doesn't mean you should procrastinate. Positive actions which are accomplished daily will not only give you a sense that you are getting a grip and solving your problems - you really will be doing that.

12

Evaluating Your Relationship:

Is It Worth Keeping?

Besides inaction, another mistake many women make is taking action without finishing a complete examination of their relationship. Often this is just from a desire to take some action, any action, to make the man stop cheating.

Inventory Your Relationship

A realistic look at the relationship is necessary to decide first whether to keep it. And if you decide to try to keep the relationship, it is necessary to identify necessary changes, not just that you should make or he should make, but changes both should make to improve the relationship.

An inventory of the relationship may also help you to see clearly. Many women, afraid they will find no one else, convince themselves that everything was happy before the cheating began when they may not have been happy at all. One way you can see clearly whether you were happy or not is to list the happy times that come quickly to mind. Then list those times you were unhappy. If the list tends to be much longer one way or the other, the conclusions should be clear. Such lists can be valuable tools to be discussed with your support group, counselor, and advisor.

An accurate examination of the relationship may often help offset the usual loss of self-esteem many women feel when they learn they have been betrayed. Looking at the relationship as a whole keeps us from focusing solely on our own faults. Everyone has faults, since no one is perfect.

Among the things you should inventory are the good things about the relationship and the qualities which are missing. Rare, indeed, is the relationship where everything one could possibly want is included. Knowing clearly what good things you have is important. Knowing what qualities are missing in the relationship can be equally as important. If you find that the list of missing qualities is quite long, while the list of good things is quite short, the message may well be that it is time to change the relationship. On the other hand, a short list of missing qualities might indicate an exceptional relationship worth saving, if it can be saved. And a fairly lengthy list of good qualities may indicate the same.

Also inventory your partner. Make a list of all his good qualities and characteristics. Then list everything you would like to change about him, including irritating habits. This list will give you an indication of your happiness or displeasure with him as a person.

Verify Your Inventory
In business, accountants are often brought in to check the

accuracy of inventories and to find errors or dishonesty. Not only may you have made errors in your inventory, but sometimes we are dishonest even to ourselves and need a second opinion. I suggest submitting your relationship inventory to scrutiny from all members of your support group.

Hopefully the opinions of others will serve the same functions it did with your self-inventory. You will cast off false assumptions about yourself. You will identify accurately if you are happy in the relationship or not. You will discover what things you find lacking in the relationship. And you may discover if you really like the man in your life or not.

Particularly important to you will be making a judgment (aided by your support group) of the chances of changing those things in the relationship you wish were different. A realistic assessment of the relationship will help you decide whether to make the effort to stop the cheating or whether to take an alternate course. This may include the possibility of ending a relationship and, in time, searching for another.

Some Important Qualities

All you have to do to verify some of the most important qualities in a relationship is gaze at the personal ads, if your local newspaper carries them. The key words for those qualities are honesty, understanding, humor, compassion, caring, and trust. Almost every woman wants these qualities in a man as a bare minimum.

Some women have other needs too. Women with children want men who like children and are relaxed around them. In these times, many women want men who can help them in their personal growth. Economic security is a major factor in a relationship, and without it, marriages can be trials. In relationships, fair sharing of expenses is important. Someone with pets will desire an animal lover. Non-smokers and non-drinkers will want the same. And it is helpful in relationships if educational levels are not too different.

Physical type is not nearly as important to women as to men but we all have a specific physical type to whom we are more attracted than others. I have known couples who broke up even though they had everything possible going for them on the surface, because they weren't happy with the other person's physical appearance. And this sometimes happens even when their physical appearances seemed perfectly acceptable, or even highly desirable, to others.

Qualities like those discussed cannot be manufactured. Either someone has them or they don't. Sometimes it takes a lifetime to create them in someone. And they are hard to teach if the student isn't willing. It is almost impossible to make someone understanding, honest, or compassionate if it isn't in their nature. It is tough to teach humor. The chances are better of adding qualities such as education.

What Kind of Relationship Do You Have?

It is sometimes helpful is to look at "the big picture." Instead of focusing on what are the good qualities of a relationship and which are lacking, imagine how the relationship works. That is, how do you and your mate interact? The following are some interesting examples of types of relationships. It is possible for a relationship to belong to more than one type.

Ideal Relationships

Ideal relationships are what we all hope for but seldom achieve.

Most of us want to be in a relationship where both partners are honest, trusting, and caring, where both partners contribute equally to the relationship on an emotional level. One problem we create for ourselves by wanting the ideal is that such relationships are often just goals, not realities. So we may spend our time judging how far we are from the goal instead of appreciating how far we might have come. And if the relationship is ideal to us, can we be sure it is ideal to our mate? Someone who feels they were in an ideal relationship will be deeply hurt if they discover their mate was unfaithful.

Romantic Relationships

Romantic relationships are those in which people feel "swept away." They just can't wait to see each other at every available opportunity. Cards, gifts, and flowers appear at every occasion. Couples that have romantic relationships often don't care where the next dime is coming from as long as they are together. In some sense, relationships dominated heavily by romance can be adolescent. But sometimes, who wants to grow up?

Alliances

Alliances are practical relationships made for money or for career advancement. In Hollywood it was common years ago for stars to marry at the urging of studios, either to cover up their personal lives or sexual preference (which might offend movie-goers) or for publicity. If you have ever read any books by Anthony Trollope you will think of "poor" upper class men wanting to wed heiresses to advance their careers. Alliances can in time work out to be sound relationships, or they may fall apart if the parties lack the necessary mutual attraction and emotional skills.

Open Relationships

"Open marriage" and "open relationships" were much discussed in recent years as alternatives. Such relationships allow the partners freedom to date and mate other than with the primary partner. For many women it is hard to conceive wanting such a relationship, while for others it may work. Most human beings, however, have great difficulty handling the jealousy. And many of us who lead very busy lives barely have time for one relationship. "Open" marriages and relationships have kept some couples together, however. Some have chosen an "open marriage" over divorce.

Dependent Relationships

In a dependent relationship, the parties are not equal. One person provides most or all of the income. Dependent persons may hang onto their relationship because they can't imagine how they will make it on their own financially. The parties may also be unequal emotionally. One party may be ill all the time, or unable to perform many of life's normal functions, such as driving a car, cooking dinner, or bathing. Both males and females can be the dependent person in such relationships.

War Zones

Some relationships are like being in battle. The man and the woman are combatants, not partners. Some couples carry on in such a fashion their entire adult lives. They may still get upset and argue over things that happened many years before. In such relationships, jealousy is frequently a weapon. One party or the other may force a divorce or separation to punish the other. War Zones are hurtful relationships that should be changed or abandoned. Usually, they can only be improved through professional marriage counseling.

Incomplete Relationships

In these relationships, one partner simply does not participate. Since the partner does not communicate when there is a problem, it is difficult to know what to do. Having a strong emotional attachment to someone who does not share their emotions with you can be a guessing game. It is better if such a game is not played. Not communicating is often a form of manipulation. It is also a way of venting anger. If you are in a relationship like this and have trouble getting out or coping, I suggest counseling.

Convenient Relationships

These take place around us all the time. Sometimes we recognize them for what they are. At other times we cloak them in romantic terms. A young college girl may live with an older man until she finishes her education. A fellow who is down on his luck may stay with a woman until he can get himself a new job. Couples stay together for the sake of the children. Convenient relationships may last if there is personal growth. Otherwise they come apart when graduation day arrives, a good job comes along, or the children finish high school.

Dysfunctional Relationships

Although "dysfunctional" can be applied to many types of relationships, here we mean those that are violent and abusive. There should be no compromise with these relationships. You must leave to protect yourself and the people and things you love. Most men who beat their wives do so because it is the quickest, most effective way of gaining control. They believe that the woman should do what the man wants, when he wants it, and in the way he wants it done. They justify what they do by the woman's behavior. They will claim that the woman provoked the beating. Even after years of group counseling, such men often revert to beating.

Relationship Changes

One person can make relationships change, but two people can do it much better. If the relationship has survived the cheating, and if you want the relationship to go on, it will help to heal the hurt if both parties see a relationship counselor. Relationship counselors can guide partners through necessary changes and adjustments. There is so much material available about improving relationships that the author has written an separate book on this subject. Lack of space simply makes the process of communication, problem solving, restoring affection, and rekindling romance impossible to discuss fully in this book. Changes made to improve relationships can be challenging, stimulating, and they can be the basis for long term happiness after cheating is forgiven.

13

Sex: Evaluating and Improving

When their partner is unfaithful, both men and women are likely to feel that they have failed as lovers. When a woman cheats, it may well be the result of some failure of her spouse, because women tend to seek out important qualities missing in their relationship when they have affairs. For men, it is not necessarily so. Some men cheat for the same reason they speed when driving—they like it. They may have a wonderful sex life at home and their mate might be the best lover in the whole world.

A relationship inventory should include some thought about sex within the relationship. Reliable Advisors can be used to dispel false notions and give helpful suggestions. If a woman is uncomfortable with her own sexuality, she should explore this with a counselor. There are counselors who specialize in sex counseling. While sex is but one part of any relationship, it is usually a very important part. Any sexual improvements may have profound effects throughout the relationship, while dispelling false notions has been proved useful in rebuilding the esteem that is lost when affairs take place.

Lack of Knowledge

Sex is a very personal subject to most women. Some have difficulty discussing sex with friends, relatives, and even their mate. Often this is merely shyness, but other times it comes from general insecurity about sex. This is unfortunate because society as a whole does not do a very good job of teaching about sex. Movies may be R and X rated, and sex may be on every television show watched. But true understanding of how one's body works is not as widespread as it should be. Many parents, themselves uncomfortable about sex, never instruct their children, or do so poorly. Some mothers frighten their daughters about sex in hopes they will refrain from it as teenagers. School boards, under the pressure of parents who either want to control sexual information or not give it at all, allow schools to skirt the issue. Good answers and honest talk are what kids need, and unfortunately many adults still need the same thing.

If there is information you do not have about sex, now is the best time to seek it. There is no reason to be embarrassed about not having complete sexual knowledge, as there are many adults who lack good sex information despite their age and success in life. One national poll recently awarded a failing grade to half the Americans taking a sex test. In fact, seventy per cent scored D or F. Now-a-days many couples have had sexual relations before they enter into a relationship but that does not mean they have knowledge.

"Normal" Sex

In general, most adults practice the same types of sex. The range of "normal" sexual activity for them includes sexual intercourse, oral sex, and mutual masturbation. This range of sexual activity is practiced by over ninety percent of couples. There is an old saying that if a man doesn't get it at home he will get it elsewhere. This usually isn't a reason for cheating since most men are getting what they want at home. Many men that have ideal relationships and great sex lives at home still cheat.

There are some women and men who will not engage in oral sex. No one should be pressured to perform any sex act they are uncomfortable with. Some women do not want oral sex for themselves because they consider themselves "too dirty." This is a false conception, since any part of the body can be washed and be as clean as another. Some women will not perform oral sex. Most men want oral sex, and this can be a problem. Prostitutes report that most men with partners at home request oral sex rather than intercourse. Some men are more understanding than others. It would be helpful if couples could agree to the range of sexual activity in their relationship before marriage, but this is rarely the case. One bashful bride, who once told her husband, "You want me to do what with that?" later could smile at her innocence. For a small number, an understanding partner is the only solution. In this chapter it may become a refrain: If there are sexual problems in a relationship, seek out a counselor.

There are some women who will not engage in sexual intercourse or prefer it as a last alternative. Unusually these women have pain during intercourse because of insufficient lubrication. There can be other physical causes as well as psychological ones. Most human beings enjoy sexual intercourse.

A physician can usually identify the cause and cure it. Women who suffer from this problem should see a physician for themselves as well as their mate. The pain could indicate a serious health threat or it could be a minor problem easily solved.

A sizeable minority of couples practice anal sex. The traditional figure has been put at twenty percent. Recent surveys have raised the possibility that the minority has grown to forty percent. It is rarely a problem if there is no anal sex in a heterosexual relationship since most men's attitude about it seems ambivalent. While curious, most men will accept the "normal" range of sexual activities. There are some men, however, for whom this is not true. Prostitutes also report a sizeable number of men who want anal sex along with other forms of lovemaking.

If there is a problem in the relationship about sexual acts, usually a counselor who specializes in sex can help. There are also educational videos which are quite tasteful covering the whole range of sexual activities. There are certainly enough books.

Impotence

There is a myth that some men are impotent and that only a certain kind of woman, someone unusually "hot and passionate," can cure their problem. Although some men do suffer from impotence, they can usually be treated successfully by medical doctors or psychologists, depending on whether the impotence is physical or mental.

Many impotent males wrongly blame their spouses for their problems. Some men become angry and abusive about impotence. Others who are emotionally impotent may cheat to prove their manhood. Men who drink to excess may also have difficulty keeping an erection or reaching orgasm.

A partner should suggest that a man suffering from impotence seek help. Impotence is a relationship threatening event.

Premature Ejaculation

The most common sexual problem is premature ejaculation. This is a problem that can be easily solved if the man will discuss it. The time required to bring on orgasm varies. There is no set rule for when ejaculation is premature. It is desirable, however, that sexual activity last until both partners are satisfied, and in the case of intercourse, premature ejaculation can be a problem. It is usually helpful to refer to a counselor who specializes in sexual matters.

Sex Drives

There are some women who would be delighted with a man who could "get it up" over and over again. And others who would be horrified. Of course there are plenty of men who cannot "get it up" over and over again. People have different sex drives. It is a rare, but lucky event, if partners have equal sex drives. Differing sex drives does not have to become a problem in a relationship. But if it does become a problem, a counselor should be consulted.

Lost Interest

A loss of interest in sex may be merely temporary if there is considerable pressure in some part of one's life. As men age, their sexual appetites decline. Prolonged lost interest more often indicates a problem in the relationship itself. If there has been lost interest, it would be a good idea for couples to talk about it. Ignoring lost interest makes one feel unwanted, undesired, and can cause loss of self-esteem. Lost interest can usually be revived with sincere mutual effort.

Birth Control

"I felt I was no good in bed at all. No matter what I did, I couldn't get Tom to have an orgasm during intercourse. Sometimes we made love for hours and hours, but nothing happened. Finally I asked him about it. He was afraid of getting me pregnant. I didn't like taking the pill and everything else was inconvenient.

What he would do was sit in his office after work on Fridays and masturbate so he couldn't climax with me later that night. I guess I'm lucky he wasn't off with some other woman."

Couples should agree on birth control practices. In Tom's case, an alternate method of birth control was picked and worked into the couple's foreplay. Disagreements about birth control, as seen in Tom's case, can lead to sexual problems and unhappiness. In extreme cases, they can lead to unfaithfulness.

Sexually Transmitted Diseases

If it ever was possible to ignore sexually transmitted diseases, it is not possible in the day and age of AIDS. There are many women who consider the risk of AIDS so great that they consider infidelity the end of the relationship. While there is always a risk of AIDS when cheating happens, the greatest risks are from those who cheat with prostitutes, homosexuals or bisexuals, or use drugs with a needle.

"I couldn't believe it. One day I had burning urination and

cramps. I thought, well, I've got a kidney infection or a bladder infection. I never would have thought I had the clap." One woman's initiation to gonorrhea was a rude message that her husband was cheating.

There is a large amount of material available in magazines and books about the current range of sexually transmitted diseases (sometimes called STD's). Information about sex is not complete without knowing what the diseases are, how they are contracted, their symptoms, and the potential long-term risk. The range of sexually transmitted diseases is not limited to the big four: syphilis, gonorrhea, herpes, and AIDS. In addition to the diseases which get all the publicity, there are a number of less familiar diseases with potential long-term health consequences. Having full knowledge of these diseases is a good idea for everyone as part of their overall health knowledge.

Good News About Sex

When we read about problems, we tend to forgot the big picture. We read the newspaper and become convinced the world is going to hell in a hand basket. Bad news is widely reported. Good news gets little attention. In the same way, we read about problems and we forget that sex is wonderful. It is a physical way that people can share their love. Education, awareness, and solving of sexual problems should make this wonderful gift even better for lovers.

14

Your Financial and Legal Position

If you are married, before you make a decision to stay in or leave the relationship, you should obtain information about your financial condition and legal rights. Without such information, you cannot make a fully informed decision.

Seeing a divorce attorney can be an emotionally wrenching step. It is unlikely the husband has been told, so it may feel as if you are betraying him. Divorce itself may be something you are avoiding thinking about. These emotional objections need to be overcome. If you are seeing a divorce attorney because your husband has been unfaithful, it is he who has betrayed you. The reason to see a divorce attorney is to become fully informed of what your finances and legal rights are in the event of divorce. One way to make the experience better might be to take a friend or your Reliable Advisor along.

Should the Husband Be Told?

Whether to tell your husband you are consulting an attorney is a decision you will have to make. One reason to tell him would be to get financial information you might not have. If you aren't prepared to confront him, it may be best to say nothing.

If there will be a check written to the attorney that he may know about, at some point you should tell him rather than let it be a surprise. Take this action before the bank statement arrives. Many attorneys, however, will not charge for an initial interview—be sure to ask the attorney beforehand. There is also free legal consultation available through many women's centers.

Do not tell your partner you are seeing a divorce attorney to scare him. Seeing an attorney, in itself, is not a threat. A divorce attorney should not become an agent of punishment. It is too expensive.

If you have to explain before or after, one possible answer may go like this. "You have made me worried about our relationship because of your actions. I am making no decisions. I am just finding out my rights."

Knowing Your Financial Condition

Many wives have complete access to all financial information in the marriage. They know the income of the husband and their net wealth. If you know, just jot the information down before seeing an attorney.

Unfortunately, some wives are kept in the dark. This is often intentional on the husband's part. And sometimes it is because of a silly concept that women don't need to know since the man is responsible for her. A woman needs to know, if for no other reason than in case something happens to her husband.

Here are two possible ways to ask for that information if you must confront your husband. "I don't know much about our finances and I was wondering if you would tell me in case something happened to you?" A more direct approach would be as follows. "You have made me worried about our relationship because of your actions. I am making no decisions. I am just finding out where I might stand if things can't be worked out. I need to know our finances."

Financial Inventory

It will be helpful to have the following financial information (or a good estimate) when you see an attorney.

1. *His Salary.* Usually an attorney would ask for a pay stub.
2. *Your Salary.*
3. *Investment Income.* Interest on savings, checking, money market, stocks, bonds, mutual funds, annuities, and some forms of insurance are typical investment incomes. Since they are all reportable for income tax as income, documents should be included with last year's tax return.
4. *Property.* An inventory of property may include a home, investment homes or summer cottages, vehicles, furniture, collectible items (coins, paintings, stamps, etc.), jewelry, stocks, bonds, insurance policies, and other valuable items. It is helpful if an attorney knows if each is titled jointly or individually.
5. *Insurance.* The types of insurance which may be important to a woman in the event of divorce, include death benefits on both husband and wife, retirement plans, and medical coverage for the wife and any children.
6. *Businesses.* If either spouse owns a business, or is a stockholder or partner in one, the value of that business could be important in a settlement. Ideally the best documentation would be a

current balance sheet and income tax return.

⑦ **Retirement Plans.** Many women do not work in business but in the home. They do not accumulate funds in retirement plans. Social security, such as it is, simply is not sufficient for most of us.

⑧ **Liabilities.** Debts may include mortgages, car loans, credit cards, personal loans, business loans, and business taxes. If a business is not doing well, there may be other liabilities with state and federal authorities.

Things You Need to Ask About

When you see an attorney, there are many things you may want to ask about. The attorney may not be able to give you an exact answer. But the attorney should be able to give you a good idea what the answer might be. Since different states have different laws, it is impossible to give you many specifics in this book. In general, however, these are the types of things you should find out.

① **Alimony.** There are different kinds of alimony. In some cases, women with larger incomes than their spouse can be liable themselves for paying alimony. Income from alimony is usually taxable. It will help to know your status concerning alimony.

② **Child Support.** In addition to how much money might be paid when, it might be helpful to know what types of custody and visitation are normally given in circumstances similar to yours.

③ **Property Division.** Nothing about a divorce, including property division, is final until the judge signs a decree. In some states, it is not final even then until a period of time has passed. An attorney cannot tell you who will keep the house or car. But an attorney can give you an idea what normally happens in circumstances similar to yours.

4) *The Process.* In addition to telling you what would be a likely settlement, an attorney can let you know what the divorce process may be like. It is helpful to know the procedure, so it isn't a shock. Without pre-knowledge, the routines of divorce, from serving a summons to trips to the courthouse, can be intimidating. An attorney should also have a good idea how long the divorce might take, depending on the husband's posture.

5) *Benefits.* Potential benefits include health insurance, retirement, and life insurance. Health insurance coverage for children should also be discussed.

6) *Disposition of Other Assets and Liabilities.* How other items of value (including investments) and debts might be resolved may be important depending on their value.

7) *Anything Else You Might Want to Know.* There may be items which require special attention. They may include sentimental items or family heirlooms, for example. Divorcing couples have been known to quarrel bitterly over household pets.

Attorney's Fees

If you use the attorney more, or if you decide to pursue divorce, be clear about fees. Many attorneys will not charge for the initial consultation (but be sure to confirm this in advance). However, when action is taken, many attorneys will require a retainer, a sum of money paid in advance, which they use on your behalf for both expenses and their fees. When the retainer is gone, they will ask you for additional money.

This arrangement may be all right if you are extremely comfortable with the attorney, but it may be better to know exactly what is being spent. Most attorneys are willing to charge you in this manner. So I suggest that each time you need legal advice or seek an attorney to do work for you, ask specifically what it will cost.

In some states and in certain situations, the husband must pay all the fees. But this is not a reason to run up unjustified bills. After all, even if he pays for it, a portion of what he pays would have been yours.

One young wife, wishing to assert her independence, proudly told her attorney that she would be responsible for her fees. Otherwise, the husband in this divorce would have had to pay her attorney fees. The young wife also proudly told her husband, who then dragged his feet to punish her. As the husband delayed, the fees quickly grew to twice what the attorney had estimated. Since the husband was not paying the fees, he had no reason to move quickly on her petition. He contested every point. She spent several years after the divorce working a weekend job to pay off her attorney.

Another wife in the same position decided to use the attorney to punish her husband. Her attorney contacted his attorney over every little detail, including who could take certain flowers from the house. When she was finally divorced, her fees took years to pay off.

If You Decide on Divorce

Only once in a while do I hear someone say, "What a civilized divorce those two had." Or "They both handled that in a really adult way." Most of the time I hear how emotionally upset and irrational couples undergoing divorce can be. One counselor described divorce to me as a period of insanity beginning several months before a divorce and lasting a year or more afterwards. I sometimes think he was not exaggerating. If you decide on divorce, you will need the full use of your support group, and I would strongly encourage use of a counselor.

Summing Up About an Attorney

You have a right to know about your finances and what might happen in the event of a divorce. This is especially important if your mate has been unfaithful. You cannot make fully informed decisions without full and accurate information.

While not underestimating the importance of an attorney in advising you of your rights and helping you to enforce them if necessary, it must be said that it is far better if a husband and wife can mutually agree to all the decisions that have to be made including property settlements and alimony. In this case, attorneys fees can be very minimal, and the attorney's role can be restricted to providing the necessary paperwork. The husband and wife, of course, will have far more money to divide. This is another important reason for attempting to maintain a reasonably good relationship with a cheating spouse even though it may be very difficult emotionally to do so.

15

Accept Your Spouse's Behavior or Try to Change It?

What Are the Options?

At some point, a decision will have to be made about what to do about the cheating, whether it is verified or only suspected. There are three general options. You can decide to leave the relationship. You can decide to accept the cheating. Or you can make an effort to persuade your spouse to stop his cheating. If you decide to try to reform the cheater, you can give him time to change, and then make a decision again about whether to stay in the relationship or not.

Some of us make good decisions by setting a certain date. On that date, we tell ourselves, our mind will be made up. Other people prefer to make a complete study of all the options before coming to a decision. Many people simply wait until the answer "just comes" to them over time. The decision about what direction you should take needs to be considered and not rushed. It may be the most important decision of your life.

What If You Aren't Sure?

Many man who are cheating will deny it if they are confronted. As one "friend" advised a cheating husband about to embark on an affair: "You have to tell her nothing is going on. Even if she finds you in bed with another woman, tell her she's hallucinating." If you aren't sure you will be told the truth, how can you be sure he is cheating? Some men are "turned in" by girlfriends, by a letter, a phonecall, or a visit. Other men are caught when seen dating by friends or by their wife. Some men talk in their sleep or "slip up." But most of the time, women are left knowing something is wrong but not quite sure what it is.

One of the functions of your support group, and particularly your Reliable Advisor, is to help you come to a reasonable and rational conclusion as to whether your spouse is cheating or not. It may also be possible to make a reasonable guess as to what kind of cheater he is. If he has been "turned in" more than once, for example, chances are fair that he is an habitual cheater.

There are some ways of finding out whether your husband is cheating which are not recommended. Here are two.

I do not recommend hiring a private detective because of the expense and the likelihood you will not get conclusive evidence anyway. Some detectives and agencies are quite scrupulous. But others may run up large bills. In any case, unless they have lots of time, and perhaps an unlimited budget, they may not find anything conclusive one way or the other. If the relationship is so bad that a private detective is needed, it may be time to end it or see a counselor. Private detectives do a lot of checking on spouses, but unlike the movies, the results are seldom so spectacular. There is also the chance of being wrong and having it discovered that a private detective was hired. This will demonstrate mistrust and will likely create very deep resentment.

Another poor tactic which has recently received some publicity must have been thought of by an attractive woman needing extra income. For a certain sum, say one hundred dollars, a wife can hire a beautiful young model to approach her man. The attractive new lady will know his schedule and find a vulnerable time to appear. She may have a flat tire or be lost. She will strike up a conversation with the man. Then she will make an indecent suggestion when she feels the time is right. The man's responses are reported back to his mate. In one case, the "dream girl" brought a husband to a motel room where his wife was waiting. Large numbers of men have failed this test. But it is hardly a realistic test, nor is it fair. And once a man has discovered that he has been deceived in this manner, he will most likely become outraged.

This book gave you a number of signs that indicate that a man is cheating. Here is an additional way of confirming your suspicions. This method may not totally confirm whether or not he is cheating, but if the mate responds honestly, it may tell you something valuable about the state of your relationship.

Sit down and talk with him. Say that you are concerned about the relationship. It just doesn't seem the same to you. Tell him why but do not ask him if he is cheating or not. Ask him if he is happy or not? And if he tells you he is not, ask him if he feels he needs space, time away from you to help him find his happiness. If you have the strength to face these answers, and if he is the kind of man who answers honestly and with concern for you, this approach may tell you if there is a problem or not.

On the other hand, perhaps you are uncomfortable doing this on your own. Maybe you are afraid of the feelings you might have, depending on his answer. Maybe he is not open. An alternative would be to have a professional, a counselor, talk with both of you. A counselor can usually determine immediately if there is a problem in a relationship. The man must be willing to participate, however, and many cheating men do not want to see someone who might find them out.

In the end, you may still have to form your own judgment with the help of your support group.

Accepting His Cheating

About half of the women in one survey said they would not consider staying in a relationship if their man was cheating. Many said "that would be the end of it." "I'd never trust him again," was another common comment. Another reaction was that since there are plenty of good men available, why put up with a cheater? Other women say they could forgive a man in certain circumstances. Usually this means just an isolated "accident" that can be overlooked. Few women say they would put up with an habitual cheater. But what is said before cheating happens is often quite different than what is said afterwards. Even wives that have divorced unfaithful husbands find themselves wanting the man back and even continuing to make love to him long after the divorce is final.

No relationship is absolutely perfect. If a perfect relationship has a score of 100, then there are other possible grades. Those grades range from zero up. Surely a woman would not put up with cheating in a relationship with a score of zero. Maybe not even in a relationship with a score of fifty. But what if the relationship scored 97 percent. Should it be abandoned because of unfaithfulness? If a relationship is truly wonderful, hopefully no cheating would occur. But what if the relationship is truly wonderful and cheating happens anyway? Some women face this type of choice. Some decide that the relationship is too valuable, too good to leave. They may try to change the man, but they also may eventually accept his cheating.

Many wives stay in relationships where there is cheating because of children or because of property. Some women care so deeply for their spouse that they simply cannot give him up. In that kind of relationship, it seems not to matter what he does, as long as she has him in the end. "We're going to be buried side by side," one woman said of such a relationship. Some very religious women believe that divorce is a sin and will stay in a relationship no matter what happens. They will always try to make it better and have faith that God will help them in the long run.

Whether remaining in a relationship with an unfaithful male is an option for you or not, every woman has a right to make her own decisions. For some women, accepting unfaithfulness is an option. We will soon deal with strategies of acceptance.

Ineffective Strategies

The strategies against cheating which have a chance of success all involve honesty and forthrightness on the part of the woman. Strategies that are based on trickery or dishonesty almost always backfire. Those kinds of strategies cause resentment and may actually complicate efforts to stop a man from cheating. Here are four examples of strategies which are usually ineffective.

Bluffing. Poker players win pots of money by bluffing that they hold better cards than they really do. There are many ways of bluffing, but none are good relationship ideas. One way of bluffing is to threaten him with divorce, financial ruin, and public ridicule. Bluffing may also be saying you have picked a strategy when you have not. For example, many women, hurt by the cheating, declare that they will do the same thing and live in an "open" relationship or marriage, when they really haven't made such a decision. I have even known women to go so far with bluffing as to send themselves flowers and spend late nights in the malls in an attempt to make their husband jealous. Bluffing strategies can backfire. When an intention is stated, then not carried out, there is less credibility the next time an intention is stated.

Competing Long Term with a Mistress. For a short time, if a man has a mistress, it may be a good strategy to show him what he will be missing. A long term competition, however, is a prescription for misery. One wife shared her husband for five years with a mistress. Only when she stopped sharing him did he drop his mistress. Competing with the mistress was wonderful for the husband. He went happily back and forth between lovers. It was probably his idea of heaven. Only when he realized he would be left without his wife did he stop. In this case, even when he came back, he would sneak off for a day or two to see his mistress again. It took several months of being back together before he dropped the mistress altogether. He only did so then out of the fear that he would lose his wife.

Sabotage. There are two ways to sabotage an affair: trick the woman, or trick the man. The mistress sends a snack sampler for his birthday, but the primary mate takes the card off and puts her own name on a new card. Sounds clever. The man does not thank the mistress for the gift, thus disappointing her. The man does thank the wife. But when the deception is discovered, there will be anger and resentment.

The mistress receives a typed invitation to meet her lover at a restaurant. When she shows up, the man is with his wife and children. Perhaps this will wake the mistress up? Will she realize she is a home wrecker? Or it will make her so mad that she will increase her competition? Sabotage can easily backfire. A primary mate might find herself a victim.

"Scorched Earth Policy." Some women maintain their anger and ignore their mate. Dinner is no longer cooked. Clothes are no longer cleaned or ironed. He is banished to the couch. No words pass between them. His old photographs and souvenirs of their relationship are trashed. If there are children in the middle, they may act as interpreters, as in, "Go tell your father what I said." Scorched Earth" is a destructive strategy. The only option to a man is to apologize and plead for forgiveness. Many men are too proud for this. There is nothing in a "Scorched Earth Policy" which promotes healing of the relationship.

It's Your Decision

You've listened to your support group. You've heard from your Reliable Advisor. You know that habitual cheaters are hard to stop. You have formed an opinion of what kind of cheater your mate may be. You have inventoried your relationship. You have met with a counselor—maybe more than one. You have talked to an attorney, if married, to see what divorce might be like. You have covered every logical step in trying to decide what is right for you.

At this point, many women are ready to make a decision to accept or attempt to change their husband's cheating behavior. Others, however, may feel they need to know exactly what might be involved in the options of accepting cheating or trying to stop it. In the following chapters, mentally "try on" each of the ideas presented to see if it "fits" well in your life and for your relationship. In matters of the heart, there are no "right" or "wrong" answers. There is only the best path to your individual happiness, and you are the best judge of what that path may be, although you will hopefully be aided by the support and advice of others.

16

The Option of
Accepting Cheating

The decision to accept cheating can be heart-wrenching. The thought that a mate is with someone else and may love someone else is difficult for most women to endure. However, the odds are with the wife. Only one man in four leaves his wife when he is cheating. The wife may prevail but she may pay a big price in pain. Only she can judge if the pain suffered is worth keeping the relationship.

There are some common strategies women have tried in order to accept cheating. All of the strategies have drawbacks, and some may be totally unacceptable. Some strategies are more likely to work than others. Each individual has to pick and choose the right one for them. Some of the alternative lifestyle choices may seem shocking to some. Yet alternative lifestyles have held some marriages together.

"Do I have to have a strategy?" Of course not. One can

simply accept what comes along. But having a strategy can be helpful in gaining control of one's emotions and putting the pain of infidelity out of mind to some extent so that life can go on.

In many cases an attempt is made to stop the cheating before accepting infidelity. Suggestions on confronting an unfaithful mate follow in the next chapter.

Ignoring It

The option to ignore a mate's behavior, or to put it out of mind, works for some women. Women who take such a strategy merely return to their normal life just as it was before they learned or suspected their mate was cheating. These women usually have faith that his cheating will not end their relationship or marriage. In many cases their reasons for accepting cheating may be practical - children or money. But others may have a very wonderful mate who meets their needs in every way but one.

There are men who have been married for decades who only cheated at certain times. Their wives "looked the other way" at these times rather than risk losing the good things their husband and their marriage offered. In what relationship is there nothing to regret or look back on with some sorrow?

Taking a Vacation

It may be that for emotional or practical reasons a woman does not want to deal with her mate's unfaithfulness at a particular time. Perhaps too much emotional turmoil has happened in her life, such as the recent death of a loved one. Or perhaps she is in the midst of changing careers and cannot afford the emotional or financial upset that ending the relationship might bring.

"Taking a Vacation" accepts the cheating for a period of time. For example, the problem is set aside until she has recovered from the death of a loved one or until the career change is made and her position secure. (In some cases it may actually be advisable to take a real vacation to a place where time can be devoted to deciding what to do about the spouse's cheating.)

It is also possible to ask your mate to take a vacation from the affair. For example, in the case of the death of a loved one, you might say, "I have too much on my mind emotionally right now to deal with this. Your behavior is hurting me and I am not clear-headed. Can we both just take a vacation for a while? I'll take no action. You be faithful." An understanding, caring mate might just "make time" for you. However, do not expect that time to be unlimited - a few months or even a few weeks may be all you can expect.

Diverting Attention

Diverting attention differs from the strategy of "Ignoring It." When "Ignoring It," a woman returns to her previous life. In "Diverting Attention" she actively pursues new interests and sets goals for herself. She diverts attention from her unfaithful mate by pursuing self-improvement. She may take the time for self-improvement from that time previously devoted to the relationship.

Many women decide to acquire a skill if they don't have one. Or they may decide to continue their education. It can also be a great time to develop talents and hobbies that have gone unused for years. Sometimes developing talents and hobbies leads to starting a business but often, if the means are available, a woman may purchase a business she has always wanted to own. In many instances diverting attention from an unfaithful spouse may result in a new career or a major life accomplishment. It is often easier to accomplish such things with the financial support of a husband's income. Husbands are often so guilt-ridden that they are willing to be very generous and supportive in return for peace at home.

Separation

Separations are sometimes used as a strategy to end cheating. "Let's live apart and see what happens." But separation is also the only way some women can accept cheating. If they were living together with their mate, there might be animosity, arguments, and the living conditions would be unbearable. Some couples separate and live apart for years without ever getting divorced. Separation can also be a good way to "try out" divorce to discover how it might be.

There are varying state laws regarding separation and marriage. Separation can occur in relationships with or without marriage. If married, you may wish to obtain legal advice first. Some states recognize legal separations and others do not. Often with divorce, financial arrangements and property settlements are influenced by what has transpired during the separation.

Separations can be more than learning experiences. For some women with domineering mates, separations can be liberating. "We may stay married, or we may not," one woman told me, "but I will never go back to the way I had to live." She also put it this way: "I like doing what I want, when I want, and with whom I want."

Maintaining separate residences may be quite expensive. Ideally the mates should agree on how the second residence will be maintained financially.

Separations may have set periods or be open-ended. If there will be visitation back and forth, some common rules may be needed.

Combining Strategies

It may be beneficial to combine any of the preceding strategies. There is nothing mutually exclusive about any of these ideas. For example, the strategy of diverting attention is frequently combined with separation.

Another possibility is that a woman knows she will accept the situation but is not sure which strategy to use. She can try out the various strategies to see which one is best for her. She can then keep strategies which make her feel good and discard those which don't.

Alternative Lifestyles

Small numbers of people have chosen alternative lifestyels to cope with cheating. However, there is very little data about the success or failure of most alternative lifestyles.

Since alternative lifestyles produce sexual behaviors which are different from the vast majority, it is usually necessary to hide this lifestyle from friends, relatives, neighbors and co-workers. This dishonesty is balanced by honesty within the relationship itself.

More men than woman have tried alternative lifestyles. The most common alternative lifestyle is "open marriage." For a while open marriages were quite popular, at least in the press, but the interest in open marriage seems to be declining. Also, men are usually more interested in participating in threesomes, swinging, and bisexuality than women.

Because there is little scientific data or research, it is hard to tell if these alternative lifestyles on the whole keep relationships together or are just preludes to their disintegration.

Before bravely departing into the world of the following alternative lifestyles, it might be wise to visit a counselor who has seen and heard everything. The evidence that an alternative lifestyle will save a relationship is scanty. Only a very small percentage of women participate in them, and there is no statistical evidence one way or the other about the effect on their happiness.

Open Relationships or Marriage

Open marriage may be workable if neither partner has any idea what the other person is doing, or if both parties are able to handle the jealousy such a relationship provokes.

This option might actually be fun for some women. It could be nice to be dating again and pursued by other men while maintaining the security of the primary relationship. Rather than suffering alone while he is out, and wondering when and if he will come home, the attention of a nice date might be cheerful. It could make up for the missing "sparks" in the primary relationship.

It may or may not be necessary to announce the open relationship to each other. It is certainly dishonest not to tell a date about the open relationship. A woman knows her mate better than anyone and will need to use her own judgment. There are also differing degrees of openness. Meeting someone for dinner after work is quite different from someone arriving at the front door for a date.

Joining In

While woman often fantasize about multiple partners, they seldom wish to act out their fantasies. Men are more likely than woman to be involved in threesomes. Only a small percentage of women ever try sex with multiple partners. Living together as a threesome is even more uncommon, but does occur.

Mistresses are more accepted in some countries than in America. Where mistresses are accepted, however, it is very rare that a threesome would come about. Other cultures accept second, and even third wives, but each marriage is separate. Even if the same house is shared, the same bed is rarely shared.

Swinging

Bobby and Bev live on a farm and would appear to be your basic everyday couple. Yet Bobby has sent an advertisement with Bev's photograph to several magazines which cater to swingers. They have been "wife swapping" with other couples and engaging in group sex for over two decades. Bobby urged Bev to give swinging a try as a more honest alternative to his philandering. For Bev, it seems to have worked. Their marriage and finances are intact.

But most women see the granting of sex as a special gift and do not want to be involved in group sex. Although most women fantasize about multiple partners, only ten percent of all women actually try group sex. For some, having group sex may be just be an experiment which is never repeated.

Some swingers appear to be slightly different types from the rest of us. They appear to be able to separate sex from love, and sexual pleasure from emotion or jealousy.

Some studies suggest that as many as twenty-five percent of men have tried group sex at least once, over two and a half times the number of experimenting women. While large numbers of men have tried group sex, the percent who practice it routinely shrinks down to a few percent or so. For most men and women it is just an experiment. Less than one in two hundred women are involved in group sex on a regular basis.

Among swingers, there are many different types. Some couples enjoy wife swapping in separate rooms. This is called "closed" swinging in the special language used in the magazine ads. Others prefer their activities to occur in the same room and enjoy watching each other or joining in. This is called "open" swinging. Some swingers are only interested in group sex, and some seek just one extra partner for a threesome, and usually specify in their ads whether this person must be male or female.

Although this lifestyle is certainly not for everyone, it does work for some people and therefore is worth mentioning. For those interested in discovering more about it, the highly specialized magazines offering this type of advertisements can be found at large newstands and sometimes at porno shops. Some of the more liberal alternative newspapers and even some of the entertainment guides and shopper newspapers now allow this type of advertising.

Beginners usually start by exchanging letters and photographs with like-minded people. Meetings are then arranged at public places, such as restaurants, where acqaintances can be made on a no-obligation basis.

Disappearing - A Very Bad Strategy

Every day, people run away from home. Sometimes they disappear with their children. They may leave no note of explanation. This will cause incredible concern. The police may be called. This is an irresponsible act, unless your safety is involved. Even if your safety is involved, your counselor may have better suggestions.

This is a very punishing action to those who do not know what has happened. It may be punishing to the innocent, including relatives and friends. Even when a note is left behind, enormous worries are created.

Some women take this drastic step to "shake up" their mates. It may have that temporary effect. But like many other acts that can "shake up" a mate, including suicide, there are always better alternatives to be considered, especially if a counselor is given a chance to deal with the problem.

Discuss Strategies With Your Support Group

It is most likely one or more of the first four stratgies in this chapter will help if a woman decides to accept cheating and get on with her life. The chances of an alternative lifestyle helping are slim but are mentioned here because they do work for some people. With the help of your support group, if it is your decision to accept your spouse's cheating, use whatever strategy helps you the most.

17

Successful Strategies
for Reforming
a Cheater

Stopping a man from cheating may be the hardest of the three options to pursue. Leaving the relationship may not be desirable, but when it is over, healing begins. Accepting cheating, through one of the strategies in the previous chapter, allows the pain to continue, but does afford some relief. But to attempt to stop cheating requires a woman to marshall her strength and her emotions, and then to make a very determined effort with no certainty of success.

Communication is the heart of a relationship and it is also at the core of successful efforts to stop cheating. The man must be willing to talk to you, or to a marriage counselor, with or without you. If he is unwilling to communicate with you or through a counselor, his cheating will likely continue, unless for some reason of his own he decides to stop.

The strategies outlined in this chapter are the ones most likely to be successful. There are other, less successful strategies outlined in the next chapter. Not every strategy may fit your situation. You will need to judge, based on your knowledge of the man in your life, which strategies will be most effective for you. Prior to trying these strategies, you will want to discuss them with your support group. You also should practice what you will say and do in conversations with your spouse, as well as his potential responses, so that you are fully prepared when you meet and communicate with him.

Communications skills are discussed in three chapters of the author's book, *BEFORE HE CHEATS: PREVENTING INFIDELITY*. There are other good books on communications available in bookstores and libraries. You may wish to practice your communication skills before undertaking this major effort.

Confronting

All efforts to change a spouse's behavior begin with the act of confronting him. In some cases, this is the only effort needed to change his behavior. In other cases, it is merely the first step of a long process.

It may be too emotionally difficult for a woman to confront on her own. Many women prefer to make the confrontation with a counselor's help.

When a woman confronts an unfaithful mate, there are three important facts communicated.

(1) She knows he is cheating.

(2) She does not want it to continue.

(3) The unfaithful male is hurting her by his cheating.

"What you are doing is hurting me and I want it to stop," are powerful words.

Many men continue cheating because they believe their spouse does not know. A few men cheat to call attention to problems in the relationship and want their cheating to be noticed. A lot of men continue cheating because they believe their spouse does not care one way or the other. What she doesn't know, these men think, won't hurt her. Those excuses to continue the cheating behavior are destroyed by confrontation.

Men react to being confronted in many ways. They may admit their cheating and promise to stop. In other cases, cheating men may deny they are cheating even when confronted with irrefutable proof. Men of high honor, whose word is their bond, may consider it honorable to deny cheating. They believe they are sparing their partner pain, and this justifies denying the truth. These men may seek a way out of the confrontation.

It is important, no matter how the unfaithful man reacts, to end the confrontation by restating. "I know I've upset you by bringing this up, and you may want to think about what I've said before we talk further. But I do want you to know that I am hurt by what you are doing and I want it to stop."

Do not add the word "please" to these requests. You are not begging. You are stating your feelings and demanding they be respected. You are justified in feeling hurt and upset about his behavior. You have a right to demand that it stop. You are being assertive and you will lessen the impact if you appear to be begging. But also take care not to become argumentative or hurtful with your words. It is not your intention to fight with him but to change his behavior.

Stating the Consequences

Stating the consequences of his cheating behavior continuing can be done during the confrontation or after it. Stating the consequences of his infidelity continuing is not threatening him. It is important that your tone and words do not convey a threat but a communication of your intentions. If he feels you are threatening him, he may become stubborn and defensive. If these are your intentions, then make them known. But never bluff. He should know what to expect if his cheating behavior continues.

There are, of course, various consequences to him if he continues to cheat despite your request he stop. You may not know what the consequences may be, in which case you shouldn't state any. But if you know that you will end the relationship if he continues to cheat, then you should tell him. He needs to know this. You should also reassure him that ending the relationship is not what you prefer.

"I do not want to threaten you. I just want to let you know what I have to do if you continue to cheat. To continue in the relationship (marriage) with you will be impossible. I will end the relationship (I will get a divorce). I don't want to do this, but if I do, it will be because you continued to be unfaithful."

Children

It is also possible that if you divorce, you may want to relocate to start a new life. This may often mean taking the children with you at some distance to him. Never use children as a weapon. Do not threaten him. But if this is a potential consequence of divorce, he should know, so he can make his own decision. There are men who might let their spouse go, especially if they are involved in a love affair, but who could not stand long separations from their children. If this possibility is likely, here is a non-threatening way to state it.

"I know you are the father of our children. I support your

right to visit them. There is a reasonable chance I will want to move to _____ in order to start a new life if we divorce. But I will always support your right to see them."

In such a manner, you may convey the point he will not see his children as much as he likes, while reassuring him you do not intend to interfere with his rights to see them. One wife, who intended to move to her parent's home more than two thousand miles away, put a dead stop to her husband's cheating by stating this consequence.

Marriage Counseling

Confronting and stating the consequences are the most effective motivators to get cheaters to stop initially. Marriage counseling is more helpful in keeping cheating from re-occurring, through improvements in the relationship. Marriage counseling can also assist in the delicate task of discussing and healing the hurt of infidelity as well as restoring trust.

Marriage counseling is heartily recommended if the male is willing to participate and be open. It may also be worthwhile to proceed without him if necessary because counselors now can provide good ideas for one spouse who wants to make her relationship work. Marriage counselors often have to cope with the problem of infidelity. Because of their experience and training, many marriage counselors can be quite skillful at opening communications and helping partners in trouble to say difficult but necessary things to each other.

Infidelity may or may not reflect an underlying problem in the relationship. The problem is often in the emotional world of the male. Wherever the cause lies, a marriage counselor can find it and help change it when it can be changed.

A woman may ask an unfaithful mate to attend marriage

counseling at the time she confronts or later. This is a decision she will need to make based on how he responds and her personal understanding of her husband. Some men will never go to counseling. Other husbands might go but never open up. There is little point in creating an exercise in futility just because it is an option mentioned in this book. Those husbands who want to participate should be encouraged. If a woman is unsure how her husband will react, then she should ask.

"I've heard that marriage counseling has helped other couples in situations like ours. I'd like to do anything that would help. I want to go to marriage counseling. I was wondering if you'd come with me?"

If he says "yes," get an appointment as soon as possible, before his interest tapers off. And be sure to carry out whatever you mutually agree to do during counseling.

Making a Contract

One tactic that many counselors use with their clients is to get them to make a contract. This contract can be verbal but it is helpful if it is written. Between partners in a relationship, this contract might be a list of do's and don'ts. Particularly for trapped males, or just unhappy ones, concessions on a woman's part may be helpful to stopping cheating. In many instances, the concessions may improve the relationship.

This strategy will not work well with a man who does not communicate. He may think the idea is "funny" or ridiculous. But if a man is communicative, and if there are things he has felt powerless to change in the relationship, a contract may be an effective tool to stop his cheating.

There are men who are very competitive and feel they must "win" confrontations. If their only option is "stop it or else" (which he might take as "stop and lose"), he may avoid making a decision about his cheating. If his option is that he "wins" and you "win," it may be easier for him to come to a decision about his cheating. Through communication, either on your own or through counseling, it will hopefully become clear what he wants that can be given in return for his renewed faithfulness.

This is a good time to remember the notes you made when evaluating your relationship. If a relationship has a lot of problems, not just cheating, it might be wise to make a contract covering all problems. Otherwise disappointments are bound to arise. Be cautious, though, not to make the terms of the contract so difficult that failure is almost assured from the start. Some people can only take so much change at one time. A good counselor can help make a contract realistic.

A contract can also start with a short period then later be changed to a longer one. This gives everyone a chance to see how practical the agreement is and to gain faith that the other person will honor the contract. Then the contract might be expanded in time and scope to a few months, or six months, or longer. This can happen gradually.

Separations

Sometimes one or both parties in a relationship need time to sort things out. A separation can be both a strategy of acceptance and of reconciliation. Separations can also be thought of as compromise solutions. They are a chance to "give it some time" before making a final decision.

Separations may be helpful with trapped males who think they want freedom but won't really know until they try it. If someone says they need time, there is no option but to give it to them. The only question is how much time, and most people unfortunately don't know this in advance.

A separation may be conducted with marriage counseling. This may aid or speed up the self-discovery process that takes place during separations.

In addition to the details about separation discussed in the previous chapter, find out how much space he wants. During separations, anxious partners tend to show up all the time with small reminders of their care and concern. It is best to find out beforehand. Constant visitation is not normally a good idea during separations.

There is also separation "etiquette" in the sense of who to tell and how much to tell. It would be a good idea to have both parties agree before hand on who to tell and what to say about the separation. This will prevent misunderstandings and possible unpleasant situations. It is very important for children.

What Happens

For most people, the decision has been made by this point. For those who chose divorce, there are a wide variety of books on how to cope, and the support group will help. For those who choose to accept cheating, one of the strategies suggested and the support group will help. For those who have made the difficult choice of attempting to stop their spouse's cheating, the journey has just begun. Maintaining a relationship for a lifetime is an ideal, but about half of all marriages end in divorce. Of the half that last, it is hard to tell how many are truly happy. For those of us who attempt to accomplish it, a healthy relationship that grows and grows is a wonderful reward in itself for whatever difficult efforts we may have made.

18

Other Strategies
Which Are
Sometimes Successful

For those who feel another strategy is needed to stop a partner's cheating, this chapter contains other strategies which are sometimes successful. These options are not for everyone. However, it is useful to read these ideas even if one does plan to use them. This is not only to be aware of them, but sometimes they will fit as an additional part to a more successful general strategy discussed in the previous chapter.

Many of the following strategies, however, are long-shots. But a woman attempting to reform a mate who has strayed needs all the suggestions and ideas she can get. Perhaps some of these will help.

Winning Him Through Romance

Many women are unable to use a romantic strategy after they

discover the man of their dreams has been unfaithful. The idea of ever doing anything romantic again with the scoundrel seems impossible. Many women rightly feel under the circumstances that they should be the one being romanced. After all, they are the ones who have been betrayed and from whom forgiveness is needed. Other woman are not so cold about using romance to win back a mate.

For those who can use a romantic strategy, it is a hit or miss thing. Usually it will not work for trapped males or with men who truly no longer love their mate. Although romance is fun for most of us, trapped males may resent romantic overtures. In many marriages, romance has been put aside for so long that is difficult to bring it back. However, romance is an important part of a relationship, and efforts to bring it back can be very positive in some cases.

It is hard not to open up any of the current women's magazines without finding a list of things a woman can do to put romance back into a relationship. Candlelight dinners, meetings at motel rooms, sexy nightgowns, dream vacations, lunches, sweet reminders, cards, surprise calls and flowers, and much more are just part of the many recommendations to put romance back into the relationship.

When couples are dating, they usually develop their own romantic signals and special gifts. They have their song, their favorite place for dinner, their most treasured vacation spot, their most important movie, etc. It can be a good addition to the strategy of romance to remember some of the "old" romantic things and bring them back into the relationship.

A few men cheat for romance and feel it is missing in their main relationship. Perhaps this strategy is best suited for them, but it can be mixed in with other strategies when there is forgiveness and renewed trust.

Sex as a Strategy

Many betrayed women are unable to forgive and forget. The idea of having sex with an unfaithful spouse is ugly and sends shivers up their spines. They feel disgusted and angry. They may, in fact, be turned off towards all men, and a bitter pill for the next man in their lives. On the other hand, some women are able to use a sexual strategy without reservation.

If sex has died in the relationship, bringing it back may help. Sex as a strategy is not a good idea in all cases. When there are love affairs, many men will enjoy the competition and refuse to decide between the primary mate and the newcomer.

One possible outcome of pursuing a sexual strategy was described this way. "I had begun to think that sex was something we did on Sunday morning, and gotten over with as quickly as possible so we could do our chores. It surprised me, but sex is fun. I'd forgotten about that."

Contrasting With His Mistress

Particularly when dealing with love affairs, it may be helpful to women with good qualities to have someone point them out to him. These may be contrasted with the mistress' poor qualities or lack of similar qualities. This task can be accomplished best by example rather than direct speech. Unless, that is, you can get a friend or relative to do the contrasting.

Waiting Him Out

Many women believe they do not need to do anything. A man will eventually change. In some cases, this is true. Everyone has a different sex drive, and some men decline in their lust more sharply than others as they grow older. Some men, who see their cheating as a personal failing, become disgusted at their own behavior. Some men, particularly in love affairs, have their hearts broken. Couples do sometimes get back together after many years. Men do sometimes regret youthful indiscretions. But does anyone really want to wait years and years for someone to change? In some cases, they do.

Religious Conversion

It is a fact that many people undergo a religious experience or conversion. Whether this is an internal psychological experience or something sent by God is a matter of belief. Judaism and Christianity favor monogamy. In mainstream American culture, then, a religious conversion may turn a formerly unfaithful man into a model husband. It does happen. And in some cases, a man can be gently encouraged to consider religion or renew a lost faith.

Some religious women may pray for intervention and conversion. They may ask others to pray. Those who believe in miracles should know that prayers may or may not be answered. In the sense that "God helps those who help themselves," religious women should augment this strategy with others from the last chapter. Many do not. Sometimes they get their miracle or get lucky, depending on your point of view.

Asking the Other Woman to Stop

Most of the time, visiting or talking to the other woman is not a good idea. The possibility that something explosive will happen during the meeting is very great. It is also likely that your actions or words will be misinterpreted or misconstrued. Visiting the other woman is often seen as an intrusion into the man's life which may be resented. Yet sometimes curiosity is too great, and many women feel drawn to learning about the other woman. And as a strategy, it sometimes works to talk to her.

One risk is that a husband may not have told a mistress he has a wife. "Jim Dandy," you say. This will break them up for sure. It may, but it may also create great resentment in the man which in the long run may prove to be an even more difficult problem in the marriage.

When a husband is cheating with a close friend, asking the other woman to stop sometimes works. It is less likely to work if the woman does not know you. It is dangerous and could backfire, but it has worked. Other strategies are safer and probably more effective in the long term.

Moving

Most of us would not want to give up friends, jobs, or the convenience of having relatives nearby. But there are times when "making a fresh start" can save a relationship. Sometimes, if the cheating is well known, it can spare embarrassment. A long move may end even a love affair. Or, the man might end up flying back to the other woman on weekends. Moving can be expensive with great risks.

Job changes may lower incomes. A woman should be sure it will actually stop the cheating and provide "a new beginning" before making such a move. With an habitual cheater, unless there are changes in him first, moving will make little difference, as he will simply start over again by finding a new partner in the new location.

Tell Him to Talk It Over With Someone

Perhaps there is one person in his life he admires and respects. This may be a relative, good friend, or someone he knows through business, church, or friends. It is very important that you do not tell that person to talk to your husband. But it is perfectly all right to suggest to your spouse that he talk it over with that person. Your husband may not even say if he talked it over with him or not. But if someone he respects tells him that he is hurting you and doing something destructive to himself, he might listen and stop cheating. There is also the danger that the respected person might recommend that the relationship with you be terminated.

Appealing to His "Better Nature"

Some men may feel very guilty about their unfaithfulness. It may be effective to say, "You are honest in all your other dealings in life. I do not understand how you can be so dishonest with me." And "You are a very compassionate man, so I hope you will stop hurting me." For this strategy to work, of course, the man must have a better nature. Most do.

19

Reforming the Habitual Cheater: It's Not Easy

A Difficult Task

Wives who set out to reform habitual cheaters face a difficult task. Many habitual cheaters have formed a life-style of dishonesty and deception. In many cases, they do not consider their behavior to be a problem. Habitual cheaters enjoy the pleasure, and often the excitement, of multiple and secret relationships.

How One Habitual Cheater Describes Himself

"I can't imagine having only one lover the rest of my life," Max M. said. Max was forty-seven at the time, a successful businessman, and admired as a good father. "I would be so unhappy if I knew I could only have one woman."

"I get tired of the same food if I have it night after night. I would get tired of the same music if I listened to it over and over. You can even get tired of desserts if you don't vary them once in a while. It's the same for me with women. I'd feel deprived and bored with only one lover.

"When I first started to cheat, I was miserable. I thought I had to decide between my marriage and other women. But I'm not miserable anymore. I know what I want. I want to always have more than one woman in my life."

Questioning Max further, I learned that he was deeply in love with his primary mate. "I'd do nothing to hurt her," he said, "which is why she'll never know about my lovers." But what, I asked him, if he was forced to choose between his primary mate and having lovers. "I hope that never happens to me," he said. "I wouldn't know which to choose. I wouldn't know what to do."

During his marriage, Max has had many close calls. It may not be true that his cheating is not hurting his wife. She certainly must wonder. She has been contacted by upset former lovers, but Max has managed to make excuses, in one case even convincing his wife the other woman had a kind of "fatal attraction" for Max. Jealous husbands have shown up at Max's house determined to have revenge, but Max was able to make his wife believe the husband had no cause. Once Max, with a girlfriend on his arm, encountered his wife in the lobby of a hotel, but because the hotel had an excellent restaurant, and this lover was a business associate, Max convinced his wife that he was there merely for a business lunch.

Men like Max are almost impossible to change. Perhaps he would stop for his primary mate whom he deeply loves, if she confronted him and threatened to leave. Most likely he would comply for a while. But Max would not be happy with monogamy. He would be miserable.

What's a woman to do, then, if she is in love or married to

someone like Max? Many women will simply end the relationship. Others assume a strategy of acceptance. But some woman refuse to give up on an unfaithful male. Their goal of stopping their husband's unfaithfulness is a hard one to achieve.

Be His Most Important Person

Habitual cheaters who have a primary relationship vary in their degree of commitment to their partner. Some are like Max, who hopes he is never confronted because he does not want to part with his wife. For a woman to have the power to change or influence an habitual cheater, she must be important to him. Hopefully, she will be the most important person in his life.

As most wives and husbands know, a successful marriage is much more than romance and sex. Those are only two very important parts. Habitual cheaters draw support and friendship from their primary relationship. Because they are busy cheating, they have little time for friendships, and their affairs cannot develop into emotional attachments without threat to their primary relationship. So wives of habitual cheaters can be very important to these unfaithful men. They can also provide a sense of security, a home base.

If a woman has decided to stick with an habitual cheater and continue efforts to change him, it will help her to be his friend. Communication should be kept open. Time to communicate may even be set aside and scheduled. Favorite activities, romantic or family, should be remembered and pursued. If a woman wants the habitual cheater to stay at home, home must be a place he wants to stay.

Difficult Questions

One woman, who has tried to change her husband's unfaithful

behavior for seventeen years, maintains that she has not adopted a strategy of acceptance. She insists she is making all efforts to change her husband, but that he is like an alcoholic or drug user who has relapses. Although friends and family have suggested that Ann leave her spouse, she will not do so. Some family members have said Ann has a romantic obsession with her husband. These are just points of view. For Ann, this is what she wants to do, even if she is destined to fail in the end. However, she hopes to succeed and enjoy a happy life with a reformed husband, at least in her old age.

I am not recommending any particular strategy for a wife to follow. It is up to the wife to decide what strategy she wants to follow. No one can make her follow a strategy she does not want. Nor should they. How she leads her life must be her own choice.

Some of the strategies Ann has tried may be useful in any attempt to reform a cheater. But they are even more appropriate for the hard-to-stop habitual cheater. These strategies are: being his most important person; giving him "space;" being friends with his friends, coworkers, and family; giving priority to family; and keeping and developing common interests. Ann has used these strategies in addition to many in the previous chapter.

"Space"

Part of making some men comfortable is leaving them enough space for their thoughts, hobbies, reading, music, or just plain time alone. Many women who have unfaithful mates feel they must be pleasing their man all the time to take him away from other women. Instead, they end up "on top" of him more than he wants. It is simple to ask if he needs undisturbed time, and it will help make his time at his "home base" more enjoyable if he needs it.

Like His Friends

A cheating male makes woman insecure, and sometimes the woman resents his friends, suspecting complicity. She will often attempt to drive his friends away—sometimes intentionally, sometimes unconsciously. This can become a further problem in the relationship. He will want to see his friends, and he will be forced to do so in a secretive way. Find things to like about his friends, and allow them into his "home base." Their goodwill could, in the end, stop his unfaithfulness. And his friends certainly are not to blame for his actions.

Learn to Like his Co-workers

Cheating males almost always have to work. They spend more time with their coworkers than they do with their friends or their primary mate. Because these people can have powerful influences on the male, welcome them into the "home base."

Give Priority to the Family

One big advantage a wife has over the various lovers an habitually unfaithful male may have, is a family that he may love very much. Cheaters appreciate mates greatly for the care given to family. The habitual cheater who has a happy family life is usually home for holidays, anniversaries, birthdays, graduations, little league games, junior and senior high school major events, illnesses, births, and marriages. This is healthy family time when he is not cheating.

Maintain Common Interests

And develop new ones. Common interests can be the cement of a relationship. They provide for additional welcome time together. Dining, dancing, and vacations are common interests which can be romantic. Home maintenance, repairs, and finances are practical bonding interests. Between couples there are so many possible common interests that new interests arise constantly.

Smooth Over Differences With In-Laws

Additional problems are not helpful in the "home base" of an unfaithful male. Welcome his in-laws, even if they are difficult and critical. Ask your relatives to minimize problems they may cause.

Sexual Addiction Specialists

In the 1980's, a new treatment for cheaters was developed based on the theory that some men are sexually addicted. This treatment was based on the idea that sex can be a powerful addiction just like alcohol or drugs. Some Hollywood stars have brought this type of treatment publicity in recent years.

Whether sexual addiction is a real physical illness, or a chosen way of behavior, makes little difference if the treatment works. If a woman is interested in exploring sex addiction therapy for her mate, she should ask a counselor for his opinion. A counselor should know if such therapy might be of benefit, and where it is available at a affordable price—some of this therapy is found at posh clinics and can be very expensive.

Many of the sexual addiction treatment programs are similar to that of Alcoholics Anonymous. AA uses a religious approach, and so do many of the sexual addiction treatment programs. Many men with secular beliefs avoid AA when they have a drinking problem, and this may be a problem with sexually addicted men if the treatment is based on a belief system they don't share. This is a factor which should be considered by the wife, husband, and counselor.

Why Habitual Cheaters Are Not Necessarily Impossible To Reform.

1. Because habitual cheaters do sometimes change.
2. Because, as men age, their sex drives decrease.
3. Because some cheaters, in mid-life crisis, decide to reform.
4. Because some cheaters, especially those with a moral background, become disgusted with themselves.
5. Because some people become saturated with sex, and decide to turn their energies in a different direction.
6. Because some men love their primary mate so much they can't bear to continue hurting her if she knows.
7. Because some men believe in monogamy and are merely in temporary emotional confusion.
8. Because some men outgrow the emotional reason for cheating, be it insecurity or a need to gather esteem.
9. Because, thankfully, we are all capable of change and betterment.

For those reasons, it would be wrong to harshly judge a woman like Ann for making a lifelong effort to change an unfaithful spouse, if that is the life she has chosen.

20

"Other Times, Other Places"

The following is an excerpt from a book in which an Asian female writer describes how a Chinese wife in Southeast Asia in an earlier part of this century dealt with her husband's repeated infidelity.*

"Your uncle tells me that he goes to Keong Saik Street every night. Those roadside flowers will wheedle every cent out of him!" Aunt Ee Poh went on and on until the tears welled up in Geok Neo's eyes. "He did not come home again last night," she sobbed.

"His big eyes roam everywhere. From woman to woman! They tell me a she-fox in Keong Saik Street has blinded him. He

*Excerpt from **Fistful of Colours**, by Suchen Christine Lim, 1993, reprinted by permission of EPB Publishers.

visits her every night!"

"What can I do, Aunt Ee Poh? You tell me. I have given him sons!"

"What you need is a concubine. A man's a man. All the same. When you are not well each month, what can he do? Naturally, he goes to look for someone else. When your uncle was young, he was like that. Until I gave him a young concubine, ah."

"But I gave him sons!" Geok Neo said, for Aunt Ee Poh had no sons.

"Aye, when a man is rich, son or no son, his heart will not stay still. A young concubine will take care of that. It is any time better than those she-foxes, I tell you.

"A she-fox, you cannot control. But a concubine, chosen by you, you can control, right or not? Listen to your old aunt. You need a concubine. Young and pliable. Someone you can bend. A char-boh-kan is best.

"A char-bo-kan (bonded servant or slave) is always below you. She can never take your place. And since you have bought her, she is yours. You can do what you like with her. And if you raise her to be your husband's concubine, eve better! She will be eternally grateful to you. In your debt, so to say, right or not? From a lowly char-boh-kan to a rich man's concubine, wah. Big jump, ah. And you have tradition on your side. Her children will have to call you mother. You will always be the mother to all the children born under your roof.

"Nowadays, ah, we are lax. In the old days, a char-boh-kan could not even go through the front entrance. Not even when she was dead. Her coffin would have to go through the back door, ah!"

On the morning of the Mooncake Festival, Ah Chun rose before dawn as usual to do the chores. The old amah came into the kitchen.

"What! Still unwashed? Go and get dressed. It is your big day today!"

Ah Chun's heart pounded with childish excitement when she donned her new samfoo suit. Such a lovely red cotton jacket. She liked the crisp feel of her red cotton pants too.

She looked at herself in the mirror. Aged 16. A woman already, Towkay-neo (rich man's wife) had told her. Ready for marriage.

The old amah hobbled into the dimly lit storeroom. "Aye, poor girl, ah," she sighed, "you have no mother to comb your hair for you. So I have to do it. May you grow white and old. May the gods bless you with sons and gold. From today your life will be different. You are going to be a married woman."

"Thank you Lan Chay. Will the master beat me tonight?" Ah Chun sobben afterwards. "I don't want to stay in his room."

"Aiyah, stupid girl! No tears! No crying today! Your auspicious day! You will count yourself lucky, ah, if you are allowed to stay in his room for one whole night!"

Ah Chun wiped her tears and looked again in the mirror. "Aiyah, hurry! You look good already. No need to look any more."

At 6:30 AM, the hour deemed auspicious by the temple medium, Ah Chun left the shophouse by the back door. No sedan chair, matchmaker, friends, nor roast pig accompanied her on her wedding walk to her master's shophouse.

She entered by the front door, hoisting a bamboo pole aross her slender shoulders.

A bucket of water hung on each end of the pole and she crossed the threshold of the house like a labourer, an apt symbol of her life to come. A bondsmaid on becoming a concubine must be reminded that she was not a pampered mistress nor an honored second wife, Aunt Ee Poh said. This time-honored ritual of carrying water would serve as a reminder that a concubine's status was only higher than that of the servants, but lower than that of the children.

Painted on the buckets were the characters for gold and silver. This was to symbolilze the concubine's auspicious entry into the family, bringing gold and silver, ushering in the gods of wealth and prosperity.

As Ah Chun stepped across the threshold, she spilt water, went up the stairs and into the living room, stopping in front of the family alter.

"Good luck is coming! Good luck and fortune, ah!" the old amah (house servant) cried. "Gold and silver spilling all over the house!"

Tall red candles and sticks of incense invited the goods and ancestors to receive kowtows (bows) and cups of wine from the new concubine.

The master and the mistress sat on two rosewood chairs in front of the alter. The master's children were the only witnesses. The master's wife, Geok Neo, had refused to spend any money on a feast.

Ah Chun stole a glance at her master. The towkay (rich man) was looking kindly at her, she thought. But Towkay-neo's face was stiff like an opera mask.

Ah Shun knelt down before them and kowtowed three times. "Towkay and Towkay-neo, please accept your lowly maid's cup of tea," she murmured.

"First kowtow, you serve and obey," the old amah chanted. "Second kowtow, you serve without delay. Third kowtow, you will bear fruit and bring them good fortune every day."

Then Geok Neo took out an embroidered slipper and hit her three times on the head. "Hitting you is reminding you who you should obey. Under my hand and under my feet, you are the concubine today." Geok Neo chanted. "Serve your master and serve me well."

"I name you Sia Liew, the pomegranate. Be fruitful and bear us sons."

That night, Sia Liew the pomegranate lay on her mistress' bed and waited in the dark for her master.

When he came into the bedroom, he said, "Take off your clothes." She closed her eyes when he grabbed her. Towkay-neo had told her that a good woman should never look at the man.

"Open wide your legs, " he growled. She clenched her fists and thrust them into her mouth. Inside her head she was screaming, "A whipping is ten times worse!" When it was finally over, he turned away and fell fast asleep, snoring.

Then the bedroom door opened and Towkay-neo came in. Sia Liew scrambled out of bed and pulled on her pants before going out of the bedroom like a thief in the night.

A bondsmaid could sleep anywhere, Aunt Ee Poh said. On the floor or under the table. And so from that night until the birth of her son, Sia Liew slept on the floor outside her mistress' bedroom.

Whenever the master wanted her, Towkay-neo would come out and awaken her with a kick. And when it was over, Sia Liew went back to sleep on the floor.

Whenever that happened, the old amah would sing softly in the kitchen, "Aye, Aye! Umbrellas have different handles, people have different fates."

Perhaps there is something of value to be found in this brutal tale. This is not to say that the plan described above is in any way good or that it is suitable for westerners in the 1990s. However, it does show that the problem is ancient and it also indicates how wide the range of possible responses might be. Some solutions will work for some people. Even ideas which seem rather extreme may find acceptance somewhere. If the story above seems bizarre or out-of-date, one only has to read a recent biography of a rock-and-roll legend to find a similar incident in which a modern Japanese wife appeased her husband's urge to philander by providing another woman. She apparently considered this a safe alternative to his compulsive womanizing.

21

Important Things to Know About Each Type of Cheater

In dealing with different kinds of cheaters, there is specific information that is helpful to know. The information given is general, and there are always exceptions to the rule. Some types of cheaters overlap boundaries and other kinds of cheaters defy categories. Knowing that each cheater is an individual, with his own life experience and complex psychological makeup, should warn us to apply generalities cautiously.

Rakes

Rakes, as you may recall, are men who can have sex at any time with any available partner they find attractive. If there is a strong primary relationship, rakes can be checked by the strategies of confronting and stating the consequences. Rakes often cheat out of deep-seated emotional needs. The needs usually can best be addressed in one-on-one counseling. Rakes do not cheat because there is anything wrong with the primary relationship.

Mystery Men

Close cousin to the rake, mystery men like the excitement of what they are doing as well as the variety of sexual experience. Their daredevil antics give them a lift which is hard to replace. A mystery man may stop cheating if his primary relationship is important to him. In order to keep him from cheating again, it will be necessary to find some interest which replaces the thrill of cheating. Cheating by mystery men is not caused by problems in the relationship but by the internal needs of the individual.

Swingers

Many swingers change their lifestyles eventually, so it may be possible to simply wait. Although some surveys put the number of men who have engaged in group sex at almost one in four (a significant number), most men don't keep at it. Group sex may be an appealing sexual fantasy, but the fantasy is often different from the reality. Some men try swinging out of curiosity, and when the curiosity is satisfied, lose interest. These men may have beeen motivated to cheat out of problems with themselves and their relationships.

There are also swingers who never leave the swinging lifestyle. Like Bobby and Bev, discussed earlier, their swinging continues for their lifetime. There is little data available on motivations or the effect on relationships. This is probably because swingers represent such a tiny minority of the population.

The Sexually Ill

Some forms of sexual illness can be cured by counseling and perhaps medication. Other types are nearly impossible to cure and the best that can be hoped is to keep the person from repeating the socially unacceptable act. Even the most sexually liberal people agree that there are certain certain forms of sexual illness. Although in different times and places, sexual practices we now found abhorrent were widely practice, our society considers acts of violence and acts with children to be especially unacceptable.

Sexually ill people are obsessed with a certain type of person, act, or sometimes both. They can be obsessed with girls who are nine years old or grandmothers who are eighty. They may want only a certain kind of sex act. Sometimes these individuals are relatively harmless to others, but maybe perhaps not to themselves. Some sexually ill people are driven to commit demeaning or violent acts, including extreme sadism of masochism.

The sexually ill need to see sex therapists and psychiatrists. This is for their own benefit, but it is also for the safety of society.

Men with such problems, when in need of help, may express themselves in unpleasant ways. One young wife was shocked to know her husband had exposed himself to her sister and asked for sex. This was an ugly event, but it was also a call for help.

While there is hope for some sexually ill people, there should be no compromise with violence or abuse. Women in such relationships, and/or children, should escape to safety, and in most cases the relationship must be ended. Outside help may keep an abuser in check.

Sexual illness usually has deep childhood roots and it is not caused by the relationship.

Homosexuals and Bisexuals

Gene is a young married professional with a baby boy. No one would suspect that he is a bisexual. Yet he has two part-time homosexual lovers who share him.

"I was just devastated," Alice said. "I mean, I could compete with a woman, but how could I compete with a man?"

The sexual preference of homosexuality is now widely tolerated. Although the scientific jury is still out on the question, it appears likely that homosexuality has biological and genetic roots.

Bisexuality is not so clearly understood or studied. There are shades of bisexuality, starting with the man who experiments once because he is curious. There are also men who will seek out gay sex from time to time at places where gay men are known to gather. Then there are men who engage in full-blown affairs with men. Over a quarter of American men have had a homosexual experience, but the number that are truly gay is much smaller. Bisexuality may represent a true sexual preference, in which case the behavior will continue. In other cases, it can be changed like other forms of cheating. Much depends on the nature of the individual.

Mistakes

Men in healthy relationships who do not have psychological problems sometimes make mistakes. Mistakes that continue are often stopped by confronting and stating the consequences. If the male is not in love, he will rarely risk losing his home and primary mate over an accident. Some mistakes may go away by themselves.

Love Affairs

Many love affairs ~~grow~~ begin as mistakes and grow from there since men tend to fall in love after sexual relations begin. Men involved in love affairs are often unhappy, torn between their primary mate and a woman they may now love. Love affairs may burn themselves out or they may go on for years.

Love affairs often arise because of a problem with the individual or his relationship. Options for stopping cheating should include confronting, stating the consequences, marriage counseling, and working on problems in the relationship.

Trapped Males

A woman with a trapped male for a husband faces some unusual dilemmas. She may have to let him go in order to keep him. She may have to grant him freedom she is uncomfortable with. Although some women might try to win him with romantic and sexual strategies, this may put additional stress on a trapped male.

Trapped males often have emotional difficulties. Making commitments is not easy for them. Perhaps, they are unsure if they want to be in relationships. Relationships are hard for them and they may dream of freedom. There may or may not be problems with their relationship. While it is good to attempt to heal problems if they exist, through marriage counseling, it may not make a significant difference. Trapped males who cheat may be stopped if they see the consequences as too painful. To make them happy in the relationship, they must feel they are not trapped. This may take some work on a mate's part, and some psychotherapy for the male. The idea of granting concessions to the male's wishes, and giving more freedom in return for renewed fidelity has proven to be effective in some cases.

Mid-Life Crisis

A man undergoing a mid-life crisis needs support. Often these are painful times of change and self-examination. A mate should participate to the extent she is welcome. Most mid-life crisis are internal affairs, and the only role left is support, if a woman can provide it under the circumstances. Some women, with just cause, have trouble being supportive if their mate has been cheating. Counseloring may ease mid-life crises. Fortunately mid-life crises don't go on forever. People in mid-life crises are uncomfortable and they need a direction. That direction may be a radical change in their life or a decision to return to old ways with renewed perspective.

A Final Word

Life can seem very tough and painful at critical moments in our lives. The comments in this chapter are meant to help. Although these comments are based on experience, interviews, and research, they are not the final word. Nor are they the only suggestions which may help. No one should limit their gathering of information about cheating solely to this book. A woman facing this problem can reach out to support groups and counselors, and seek further ideas from other books and articles. It is important to find the solution which best matches your own personal situation. An open attitude, and a willingness to adapt, will be helpful in handling such a major challenge in life.

Afterword

No matter what decision you reach about cheating, you will want to make extensive use of your support group. Some relationships are just too painful to continue and in these cases, divorce is the only answer. If this happens, remember that one half of all American women go through this experience at least once. There is help available from many sources, including self-help books. Some relationships may be too valuable to lose over cheating. Use the opportunity for personal growth, and strive so the result will be a strengthened relationship.

Some Helpful Ways to Think of the Problem

1. You are not alone. Estimates of how many men cheat range from around half to three-quarters.

2. There is nothing wrong with you. Most men usually

cheat because of their own emotional needs, upbringing, and possibly their biological natures.

3. You can do something about cheating. You have many options. You can improve your life and maybe your relationship. You need to explore your options and pick the one that is most suited for you.

4. You have not failed. If anyone has failed, it is the cheater. But perhaps no one has really failed. Most likely, it's just something unpleasant that has unexpectedly happened and has to be dealt with.

5. You can accept this as a challenge to possibly improve your relationship, and certainly to improve yourself.

6. In time, things will get better.

7. You will survive this problem. Millions of other women have not only survived, but improved their lives in the process.